MW00719198

Critical Theory and Practice in Psychology and the Human Sciences

Series Editor
Tod Sloan
Lewis & Clark College
Graduate School of Education and Counsel
Portland, Oregon
USA

This series offers titles that challenge the dominant models of psychological science and their applications in order to foster social transformation toward equity and justice. With this common aim, various forms of critical and liberation psychology have emerged over the last few decades, drawing on neo-Marxism, poststructuralism, critical hermeneutics, feminist psychoanalysis, queer studies, and postcolonial thought. Critiques grounded in these perspectives reveal the ideological functions of mainstream theories and the therapeutic, organizational, and educational practices that flow from them. Titles in this series explore these links between theory and practice and argue for progressive alternatives. Critical Theory and Practice in Psychology and the Human Sciences publishes bold and innovative monographs that advance critical psychology and propose socially transformative practices. The series welcomes submissions from a range of theoretical perspectives and disciplinary orientations, including clinical psychology and counseling, social work, community psychology, organizational development, and activism.

More information about this series at
http://www.springer.com/series/14941

Robert Samuels

Psychoanalyzing the Left and Right After Donald Trump

Conservatism, Liberalism, and Neoliberal Populisms

palgrave
macmillan

Robert Samuels
UCSB, Santa Barbara
California, USA

Critical Theory and Practice in Psychology and the Human Sciences
ISBN 978-3-319-44807-7   ISBN 978-3-319-44808-4 (eBook)
DOI 10.1007/978-3-319-44808-4

Library of Congress Control Number: 2016950847

Cover illustration: Pattern adapted from an Indian cotton print produced in the 19th century

Printed on acid-free paper

This Palgrave Macmillan imprint is published by Springer Nature
The registered company is Springer International Publishing AG
The registered company address is: Gewerbestrasse 11, 6330 Cham, Switzerland

CONTENTS

CHAPTER 1

Introduction

Abstract This book uses psychoanalytic theories and practices to explain how someone like Trump can rise to power and why liberals have failed to provide an effective political alternative. In looking at the 2016 campaign for the presidency of the United States, I discuss how the liberal (Clinton) abandonment of the working class has resulted in a populism of the Right (Trump) and the Left (Sanders). These dynamics cannot be understood solely in terms of economics and politics, and so it is necessary to turn to psychoanalysis to see how the fantasy of victimhood unifies the Right and why moderate Democrats have moved away from their support for workers and a more equal society.

Keywords Trump · Liberals · Conservatives · Psychoanalysis · Clinton · Democrats · Conservatives · Obsessional narcissism · Populism · Unconscious · Freud · Lacan

This book does not attempt to interpret Donald Trump's unconscious or the sexuality of any politicians.[1] Instead, I use psychoanalytic theories and practices to explain how someone like Trump can rise to power and why liberals have failed to provide an effective political alternative.[2] In looking at the 2016 campaign for the presidency of the United States, I discuss how the liberal (Clinton) abandonment of the working class has resulted in a

© The Author(s) 2016
R. Samuels, *Psychoanalyzing the Left and Right After Donald Trump*,
Critical Theory and Practice in Psychology and the Human Sciences,
DOI 10.1007/978-3-319-44808-4_1

1

populism of the Right (Trump) and the Left (Sanders). These dynamics cannot be understood solely in terms of economics and politics, and so it is necessary to turn to psychoanalysis to see how the fantasy of victimhood unifies the Right and why moderate Democrats have moved away from their support for workers and a more equal society. Moreover, it is the liberal fear of the radical Left and the populist Right that often serves to demonize a real push for social and economic justice. In what I call the pathology of obsessional narcissism, we discover the unconscious roots of the liberal investment in an illusionary meritocracy, which replaces a political focus on poverty, labor unions, and the working class with an emphasis on education as the solution to most social and economic problems. Although Bernie Sanders appears to represent a true Left alternative, I point to the limitations of his populist policies and politics. I also argue urgently that in the age of multinational corporations and global climate change, we need a new model of global justice and government that requires an understanding of analytic neutrality and free association.

In looking at the work of Freud, Lacan, and the psychoanalytic critic Slavoj Zizek, I place the current state of American politics in a larger global context. While much of my analysis deals with the 2016 U.S. presidential election, I also examine how we are seeing the same pattern repeated throughout the world (i.e., Brexit): as the Left fails to provide a real alternative to global capitalism, displaced workers blame immigrants, people of color, and Muslims and end up supporting far-Right political ideologies. Meanwhile, moderate liberals remain tied to outdated policies as their fear of the Left and the Right pushes them to conform to the status quo, and all of these political positions fail to confront the current need for a global form of justice and government to deal with problems like climate change, inequality, terrorism, and multinational capital.

OUTLINE OF CHAPTERS

Chapter 2 argues that we cannot understand aspects of the current conservative backlash movement if we do not comprehend the role played by fantasies of victimhood. In turning to Freud's original insights into hysteria and masochism, I show that victim identification is one of the strongest political forces in the world today. Not only do religious fundamentalists base their identity on real and imagined scenes of victimhood, but after 9/11, the strongest countries in the world were able to present themselves as victims, and as we learn from psychoanalysis, victims always see themselves as innocent and pure as they reject all criticism and justify all vengeful hostility.

Just as nations and religions define themselves through victim identifications, the wealthiest people in the world have been able to reimagine themselves to be the victims of taxes, government, and liberal institutions like universities, unions, and mainstream media. I show in this chapter that by affirming the mental autonomy of the unconscious and the fundamental masochism of the subject, we can better understand the underlying paranoid fantasies that structure conservative ideology and global politics. Furthermore, I argue that psychoanalysis can also offer a critical counter-discourse to the rise of fundamentalism and neoliberal conservatism.

Chapter 3 turns to a psychoanalytic understanding of the liberal aspects of neoliberal politics. Using Freud's theories of transference, narcissism, and obsessional neurosis, I posit that liberals often want deny their own aggression by having their ideal self-recognized by an ideal Other, and so they often cling to a rhetoric of progressive moral righteousness as they engage in destructive acts of competitive capitalism. As Freud discovered through his experience with transference, patients will idealize their analyst so that the analyst idealizes the patient, and this type of relationship sets of a narcissistic form of social conformity. Since liberals want to be seen as ideal by an ideal Other, they cannot tolerate criticism or acknowledge their role in destructive social processes. In developing the concept of obsessional narcissism and analyzing Hillary Clinton, I examine how psychoanalysis explains many of the contemporary failures of liberalisms. I also indicate how progressive social movements can avoid the pitfalls of narcissistic transference by creating political organizations that move beyond identification, idealization, and cynical conformity.

Chapter 4 argues that if we want to fully understand the political popularity of people like Donald Trump, we should return to Freud's theory of the group formation and his notion of emotional identification. As a form of group hypnosis, Right-wing populism relies on followers suspending their critical faculties as they access parts of their unconscious id, and psychoanalysis helps us to understand how these unconscious processes function in political movements. Moreover, Freud's theory of free association allows us to see the ways Trump's campaign might, in one sense, actually be good for America because it serves to expose the underlying fantasies that support the conservative coalition. Finally, it is important to place Trump's persona in the context of contemporary media and neoliberal capitalism.

This critique of Trump's populism of the Right is matched with an analysis of Bernie Sanders' populism on the Left. Although Sanders offers a much more hopeful and progressive vision, his promotion of a fake revolution and false socialism reveal the limits of neoliberal progressive politics. In failing to take on the global foundation of economics, politics, and culture, Sanders presents a series of policies that are unable to deal with climate change, inequality, terrorism, and taxation. As one of the most famous Left-oriented economists in the world, Thomas Piketty, has argued, the only solution to our current system of capitalist inequality involves a global wealth tax, and yet Piketty himself never mentions the need for a global system of government in order to implement such solutions.[3]

Chapter 5 argues that we have to rethink the limits of nationalism as we recognize the need for a global government to confront the global challenges of climate change, financial capitalism, tax avoidance, terrorism, migration, and international poverty. By returning to the Freudian concepts of free association and the neutrality of the analyst, I offer a model for global solidarity and universal human rights. Furthermore, since most of our current social issues are global in nature, I argue that we need a global solution in general, but global solidarity is blocked by narcissistic nationalism and the capitalist death drive. In examining contemporary social movements for global justice, I articulate a theory of universal social solidarity.

Notes

1. I completed writing this book in June 2016 before the Democratic and Republican conventions.
2. For the last three decades, I have been going to conferences and reading books that try to establish the political significance of psychoanalysis. One of the most striking things I have encountered over and over again is that many of the contemporary proponents of psychoanalysis do not have a strong grasp of the specificity of psychoanalytic theory and practice. A major claim of this book is that there is a small set of fundamental principles that define psychoanalysis, and these principles can play an important role in helping us think about *and* change politics in the age of Neoliberalism. The four basic concepts that I will be discussing throughout this book are the unconscious, free association, transference, and the drives, and I will argue that almost every other concept related to

psychoanalysis is either a distraction from or a component of these four major concepts. Moreover, I will position psychoanalytic discourse as a supplement to other social science theories. From this perspective, psychoanalysis adds something that is lacking in the fields of economics, political science, sociology, anthropology, psychology, and history.

3. Piketty, T. (2014). *Capital in the twenty-first century.* Cambridge, MA: Harvard University Press.

CHAPTER 2

Victim Politics: Psychoanalyzing the Neoliberal Conservative Counter-Revolution

Abstract This chapter argues that we cannot understand aspects of the current conservative backlash movement if we do not comprehend the role played by fantasies of victimhood. In turning to Freud's original insights into hysteria and masochism, I show that victim identification is one of the strongest political forces in the world today. Not only do religious fundamentalists base their identity on real and imagined scenes of victimhood, but after 9/11, the strongest countries in the world were able to present themselves as victims, and as we learn from psychoanalysis, victims always see themselves as innocent and pure as they reject all criticism and justify all vengeful hostility.

Keywords Victim · Fantasy · Conservative · Identification · Masochism · 9/11 · Fundamentalism · Israel · Imaginary · Ego · Mirror stage · Freud · Lacan

This book argues that we need psychoanalysis to help us understand and work against neoliberal political ideologies and practices. Without the key theories that Freud developed and Lacan clarified, it is hard to explain how wealthy people have been able to represent themselves as victims and why the real victims, workers with stagnant wages and limited opportunities, have identified with the rich.[1] To comprehend

© The Author(s) 2016
R. Samuels, *Psychoanalyzing the Left and Right After Donald Trump,*
Critical Theory and Practice in Psychology and the Human Sciences,
DOI 10.1007/978-3-319-44808-4_2

and work through this ideological structure, we need to affirm some of the basic insights of psychoanalysis concerning fantasy, consciousness, object relations, and identification.

IMAGINARY POLITICS

The French psychoanalyst Jacques Lacan created the concept of the Imaginary order to show how individuals tend to see the world as a dyadic relationship between the self and the other.[2] From this perspective, either I am content because I have the object of my desire, or I am frustrated because I imagine that the other is fulfilled and has the object I desire. This Imaginary relationship is then fundamentally dualistic and helps to explain feelings of envy, rivalry, and jealousy. Moreover, Lacan calls this structure Imaginary because our sense of completeness and fulfillment is derived from the way the ego comes into being in infancy by identifying with a complete image of a body in a mirror or mirroring relationship. By seeing our bodies in the mirror as being complete and whole, we internalize a desire for unity and coherence, and any time our fulfillment is threatened, we blame others for undermining our desired unity.

When we turn to contemporary politics, we see that the dominance of Imaginary duality often structures the subjectivity of neoliberal politics. In the case of contemporary conservatives, the underlying structure is that the isolated individual (ego) resents having to sacrifice for society (the Other) and feels that the other is stealing his or her freedom and enjoyment.[3] In other words, there is a fundamental irrationality that drives our political discourses, and very little will change if we do not find a way to counter the use of the Imaginary for destructive purposes. To help clarify this situation, we can look at Thomas Frank's *Pity the Billionaire: The Hard-Times Swindle and the Unlikely Comeback of the Right*. I turn to this book because this well-known political analyst focuses on the irrational logic of the conservative counterrevolution, but he cannot explain his own explanations since he lacks a psychoanalytic understanding of Imaginary fantasy.

Throughout this book, I will be defining neoliberalism as a political ideology centered on the privatization of public institutions, the promotion of free market fundamentalism, a tax revolt led by wealthy people and corporations, and the globalization of capitalism, labor, and media. This movement has been led by a conservative counterrevolution, but it also has been supported by liberals and progressives.

In this chapter, I focus on the ways that the conservative coalition in America has used an Imaginary mode of victim identification to promote a neoliberal agenda.

FRANK'S PITY

In describing the Great Recession of 2008 and the political and social reactions to this event, Frank focuses on how instead of responding to the financial meltdown with new governmental regulations and aid to the devastated middle class and working class, conservatives from all class groups appeared to show pity for the perpetrators of the economic collapse: "This was no ordinary business-cycle downturn. Millions of Americans, and a large number of their banks, became insolvent in a matter of weeks. Sixteen trillion dollars in household wealth was incinerated on the pyre Wall Street had kindled. And yet, as I write this, the main political response to these events has been a campaign to roll back regulation, to strip government employees of the right to collectively bargain, and to clamp down on federal spending... Before this recession, people who had been cheated by bankers almost never took that occasion to demand that bankers be freed from 'red tape' and the scrutiny of the law. Before 2009, the man in the bread line did not ordinarily weep for the man lounging on his yacht" (p. 3). The first thing Frank struggles to explain is why did so many people react to a great financial disaster by feeling pity for the people who caused it and profited from it. To be precise, we must ask how did the wealthy position themselves as victims, and why did the real victims sympathize with the false victims?[4] Moreover, it is important to look on a global scale to examine why this financial crisis resulted in policies of austerity and anti-immigration instead of a call for more public intervention and regulation.

Using Lacan's theory of the Imaginary, we shall see that neoliberal conservative political ideology often functions by catering to a dual conflict between the individual and all others. In this structure, the world is divided into victims and perpetrators, and the victims are always pure, innocent, and right, while the perpetrators are impure, guilty, and wrong. Here, the ego functions as a symptom in the sense that the harmed self uses suffering to manipulate others and to form a solidified identity. Drawing on Freud's theories of masochism and hysteria, Lacan posits that suffering justifies the aggression and resentment of the self-identified victim. However, political ideology has to be combined with individual psychology since the Imaginary definition of the victim and the perpetrator is determined by the social definitions of purity, innocence, and righteousness: only the innocent victim deserves our pity, and society determines who is innocent and who is guilty.

The great ideological trick of the neoliberal Right has been to reduce every relationship to an Imaginary dual relationship and to define who are the victims and who are the perpetrators. Thus, conservatives have spent decades convincing the public that the real perpetrators are not wealthy people and corporations but the cultural elites: "And their conservative wing had a coherent theory to tell the world. Everywhere you looked, they declared, you saw a colossal struggle between average people and the 'elites' who would strip away the people's freedom."[5] The first rhetorical and psychological move of this conservative counterrevolution, thus, was to define the perpetrator in terms of cultural issues: the elites are the liberal government, media, and professors and not the multinational corporate leaders or the millionaires and billionaires. However, what Frank and others cannot explain is how does this ideological reversal work, and why do many people buy into an interpretation that is clearly against their own self-interest. It is therefore essential to ask what are the cultural and psychological mechanisms allowing people to invest into this ideology besides a lack of knowledge of systemic issues?

Turning to Freud's early work with hysterical patients, an important lesson that psychoanalysis can teach us about the conservative counter-revolution is the idea that people fantasize about their own victimhood, and this fantasy helps to frame how they see their world and their own identity.[6] One of Freud's big moves here was his controversial discovery that many of the women he thought were abused by their fathers may have actually fantasized about their victimization.[7] This turn away from the so-called "seduction theory" is very controversial because it appears to blame the real victims of abuse, while it removes the real abusers from any responsibility. There has been much written on this change in Freud's theory, but what is often missing is the question of why people might fantasize about their own abuse and what does it mean that we can often never know for sure if a scene of abuse is real or imaginary?

Freud's first patients were women who suffered from physical ailments that did not make medical sense. For example, a woman would not be able to use part of her arm, but the other parts appeared to work fine. Freud discovered that medical knowledge could not explain these symptoms, and so they must have a psychological cause.[8] He soon realized that all of these patients claimed that they were abused by their fathers, and their symptoms were connected to the traumatic scenes of "seduction." For instance, a woman who had a hard time breathing was touched on the neck during a sexual assault; she then remembered the repressed traumatic event by marking it by a bodily pain, which she herself did not understand. Freud thus saw the hysteric's symptom as a sign of a repressed trauma, and he soon found that if the memory of the event was rediscovered in speech, the symptom would go away. This is how psychoanalysis was born, but Freud started to suspect that some or all of the alleged assaults did not happen in reality; instead, they must have been imagined.

In his rereading of Freud's case of Dora, Lacan is able to reveal how Freud had an early insight into the ways hysterics use pain and suffering as a way to manipulate others.[9] Employing Hegel's concept of the Beautiful Soul, Lacan argues that Dora denied her own role in the social relationships that exploited her, and she sought to maintain a front of innocence to protect not only herself but all of the people in her exploitive environment. One of the things we learn from this interpretation is that the Imaginary fantasy of victimhood allows the victim to maintain a sense of purity and innocence, while all vengeance is justified. Once again, it is important to stress that psychoanalysis does not deny the traumatic nature of real assaults; rather, what is emphasized in analysis is the possibility of Imaginary fantasies of victimhood.

Stepping back and looking at contemporary politics, we find that the fantasy of victim identity is one of the most powerful political forces in the world today. Not only does victim identity explain how powerful nations, like the United States, are able to attack others and still feel innocent and pure, but it also explains why the most powerful people in society can represent themselves as disempowered, while they attack the poor, immigrants, and people of color for being victimizers. It is also vital to point out that most religions have centered their identity on scenes of victimhood, and this type of Imaginary identification allows for a combination of self-righteous purity and justified vengeance.

Without the psychoanalytic theory of Imaginary fantasy, it is difficult to explain the political identification with selected victims and perpetrators. Not only does Freud's work articulate how pain is turned into pleasure and how fiction is combined with reality, but his theory of identification helps us to understand how ideology is able to function. In *Group Psychology and the Analysis of the Id*, he makes the provocative statement that hysterics bond over their shared sense of victimhood.[10] What then helps to explain why people buy into the conservative counterrevolution is that they are identifying with the shared emotion caused by their individual sense of Imaginary victimization.

In returning to Frank's analysis of contemporary politics, we see that this shared fantasy of victimhood is coupled with an underlying fantasy of total freedom and enjoyment: "Economics have become the latest front in the culture wars. The issue, the newest Right tells us, is freedom itself, not the doings of the subprime lenders or the ways the bond-rating agencies were compromised over the course of the last decade."[11] In order for the wealthy elites to show that they are the real victims of contemporary society, they not only have to define cultural elites as the true perpetrators, but they also have to feed into an underlying fantasy of total freedom. In other terms, in the conservative celebration of the individual's right to keep all of their money and not be regulated by the government, we find an Imaginary fantasy of the ideal ego which does not need the other and sees the social Other as threatening castration. Just as Freud argued that hysterical symptoms are always constructed out of two contrary fantasies, we see that the fantasy of victimization is coupled with a fantasy of unlimited power and freedom.[12]

Throughout his *Civilization and its Discontents,* Freud gives several explanations for this fantasy of total freedom and power. One of his theories is that we all experience an initial state of primary narcissism, which makes us feel that we have unlimited autonomy.[13] This Imaginary fantasy of unrestricted enjoyment and freedom can also be explained by Freud's early theory of the primary processes where one simply hallucinates the satisfaction of one's wishes, and therefore, the primary original state of all humans is one of total self-satisfaction.[14] What Freud calls the pleasure principle is the notion that our minds give us the ability to imagine a world of total fulfillment, and any restriction to this satisfaction is seen as an external threat that has to be rejected, repressed, or internalized.[15]

This theory of the underlying Imaginary fantasy of freedom and enjoyment helps to explain why conservatives feel that any level of governmental regulation or taxation is a direct threat to their identity: from the perspective of primary self-satisfaction, society itself is a form of castration and persecution. In fact, Freud's myth of the primal horde from *Totem and Taboo* can be read as a historical fantasy that narrates the loss of our Imaginary enjoyment.[16] According to the story Freud borrowed from Darwin, at first there was an all-powerful father who had access to all of the women and denied his sons any enjoyment.[17] The brothers then banded together and killed off the father and formed the first society. Psychoanalysis thus always posits an initial fantasy state of total power and enjoyment, which later has to be given up through an act of sacrifice and victimization.

One reason then why the rich feel they never have enough money and power and why they consider all government regulations and taxes as being assaults on their freedom is that they hold onto an underlying, unconscious fantasy of unlimited freedom and enjoyment. Like a hysterical symptom, conservative ideology combines the Imaginary fantasy of self-satisfaction with a fantasy that translates social interventions and regulations into victim identifications to produce a political rhetoric of reversed victimhood. As Frank rightly points out, in this conservative discourse, freedom is often equated with the free market: "Now, there is nothing really novel about the idea that free markets are the very essence of freedom. What is new is the glorification of this idea at the precise moment when free-market theory has proven itself to be a philosophy of ruination and fraud. The revival of the Right is as extraordinary as it would be if the public had demanded dozens of new nuclear power plants in the days after the Three Mile Island disaster; if we had reacted to Watergate by making Richard Nixon a national hero."[18] Frank here appears to be astounded by the ability of the Right to hold onto the mythology of the free market, and we can explain his incomprehension by his failure to grasp the irrational and fantasy-based nature of political ideology. From a psychoanalytic perspective, the very notion of a "free" market is an unconscious fantasy, which is not the product of reason or rationality.

Another problem that Frank continuously bumps his head against is the way that the Right is able to escape all criticism when they make their irrational claims about the free market: "To insist that the free-market creed is beyond ideology might sound like the baldest sort of propaganda today, but all through the eighties, the nineties, and the zeroes our leaders whistled that happy tune, congratulating themselves for figuring it all out. Those were the golden years of libertarianism, a time when our choice and master spirits agreed on the uselessness of big government and took the benevolent rationality of markets for granted."[19] As I argued above, for conservatives, the free market and the elimination of government intervention allow for a return to the primary fantasy of total freedom and total enjoyment like the all-powerful enjoying father before the brother's organize to kill him and make him share all of the women. In fact, one of the irrational aspects of this libertarian fantasy of the primal free market of total freedom is the idea that markets are natural and not the result of concerted social action. This ideology relies in part on the mythology of the Invisible Hand and the idea that markets are self-regulating and do not require governmental intervention; however, the belief in the Invisible Hand itself only works by reactivating the primary fantasy of the totally free and enjoying self-satisfying id.

As Frank stresses, a vital rhetorical move in this naturalization of the market is the notion that it represents a nonideological ideology. In other words, conservative ideology has to pretend that it is just reinstating a natural order, and therefore it is not part of an artificial social system organized by individuals working together. In many ways, this ideology has to reject the psychoanalytic principle that we are not natural beings since all of our desires and drives are shaped by language and social systems. Psychoanalysis also tells us that one of the ways social structures get people to buy into oppressive systems is through the social production of the "natural": in other terms, society defines what is outside of the social realm, and people trying to escape social control see this produced outside or other as a source of freedom. For example, human sexuality itself is shaped by culture and history, and yet society treats it as natural and real. Freud's theory of the drives then represents a break with instinct and nature by showing how sexual desire is linked to transgression, social guilt, shame, and prohibition. Moreover, we can understand the headless, heedless global capitalist drive for more money and power as deriving in part from the insatiable drives, as described by Freud, that unlike instincts do not have a predetermined object or aim.[20]

Not only do many neoliberal conservatives buy into the ideology that the free market is the natural state of human interaction and exchange, and to limit the free market would be akin to castrating the primal enjoying father and cutting off our natural instincts, they also believe that evolution determines the free market and naturally selects out winners and losers. For example, Frank argues that when the government was considering helping out people who lost their homes and their savings in the United States, many of the victims of the financial crisis turned around and joined the Tea Party movement and attacked the government for trying to interfere by helping out the losers who were selected by the natural economy: "The Tea Party movement started with the desire to punish the losers of society who had taken on bad mortgages, and not the wealthy business people who designed the fraudulent financial instruments. What has to be explained is this resentment shown towards the real victims of the crisis. Why did poor and middle-class people who were being devastated by the financial crisis turn around and blame poor and middle-class homeowners? Perhaps we can find the explanation in the idea that there can only be one true victim, and if the victims are the people who are paying taxes to the wasteful, intruding government, then the victims cannot be the ones harmed by the criminal financial class."[21] One of the things that Frank highlights here but cannot quite explain is the idea that there can only be one class of victims. With a deeper psychoanalytic understanding, he would realize that an aspect of victim identification involves the splitting of the world into good and bad objects. Therefore, in order for the self to be experienced as all-good, it must see others as being all-bad, and this binary division feeds off of the social construction of political classes and the naturalization of social hierarchies. For example, by defining the government and people receiving public assistance as naturally bad, there is no space to understand that the real abusers of the system were the financial institutions that produced fraudulent loans and gambled on their own inflated investments. Political polarization then feeds into the fantasy structure of victimhood by clearly dividing the world into victims and perpetrators.

A Brief History of American Victimhood

As Alyson Cole argues in her *The Cult of True Victimhood*, in order for the victim to gain support and sympathy, the persecuted person has to be represented as being morally just and pure.[22] Cole describes that throughout American history, there has been a shifting of who qualifies for the position of the innocent victim and who becomes labeled as the oppressive persecutor. America started by not only victimizing Native Americans, but by declaring that the colony was a victim of British taxation. Moreover, the United States has often represented itself as the home for people who are escaping persecution from around the world, and at the same time the United States enslaved African Americans and killed Native Americans, and it tried to maintain a self-image of being innocent and pure.

Cole shows that during the recent period of neoliberalism, as the Right blamed the Left for catering to minority victim groups through welfare programs, the Right began to represent itself as the true victims of liberal American society.[23] Then, in response to the shift in victim identification, the New Democrats, like Bill Clinton, openly argued that minorities had to shed their victim status and welfare had to be reduced.[24] Both parties thus bought into the neoliberal conservative strategy of justifying the reduction of government, and therefore justifying a reduction of taxes, by equating Big Government with welfare programs. Furthermore, the Right has argued that welfare only serves underserving minority "welfare queens," and this type of social program is no longer necessary because racism is now over. To prove this final point, the Right had to argue that discrimination was only an Imaginary injury created by liberals and internalized by minorities in order to justify the expansion of the welfare state and the increased need for taxes and government. According to the neoliberal conservative ideology, liberal professors, media, and politicians are the real persecutors because they make the wealthy pay for unneeded programs, while the liberal class attacks everyone for harboring racist, homophobic, and sexist thoughts.

A key aspect then of political discourse is the ability of a particular coalition to define the perpetrators and the victims, and in this case, the Right was much more effective: "But it was the Right that grabbed the opportunity to define the debate, using bailouts to shift the burden of villainy from Wall Street to government."[25] Here we see how political ideology works with fantasy structures: by clearly defining the roles of the perpetrator and the victim, the political class activates Imaginary dynamics. What is interesting to note is that Leftist scholars like Ernesto Laclau argue that real social movements can only take hold if they are founded on a clear antagonism between the victims and the perpetrators.[26] I will later show how this oppositional strategy is self-defeating because it ultimately serves to feed destructive Imaginary fantasies and identifications.

THE POLITICAL IS PERSONAL

Another important function of political fantasy structures is that they help to make ideological constructions personal. Imaginary fantasies frame how people see reality by turning social formations into perceived personal experiences. In the case of the conservative counter-revolution, there is often a move from thinking about politics through statistics and systemic understanding to focusing on anecdotes and isolated private individuals. What makes this aspect of fantasy Imaginary is the ego of consciousness divides the world in two and sees things only from the perspective of the isolated individual confronted by a hostile external world.

In speaking to many conservatives, I have been surprised to discover that they really experience their lives through the lens of victimhood. Even very wealthy people see themselves as victims of taxation and governmental regulation. I used to think that they were only mimicking a political ideology to justify inequality and the cutting of taxes, but I found that they actually live their lives as victims. Their relationship to reality is therefore not based on reason or direct perception: they have an Imaginary relationship with their own experiences, and they live this fantasy frame as if it is a direct, natural perception. As Lacan argues, consciousness is defined by Imaginary fantasy and the splitting of the world into the good self and the bad other. Since according to Lacan, we first gain a sense of self and bodily unity by identifying with an image in the mirror, fantasy is itself always Imaginary and narcissistic.

Returning to Frank, we see how Imaginary fantasies shape the conservative counterrevolution: "Whenever our tea-partying friends warm to the subject of letting-the-failures-fail—and they do so often—sooner or later they inevitably turn from the bailed-out banks to those spendthrift 'neighbors' identified by Santelli, those dissolute people down the street who borrowed in order to live above their station. These are the failures who need to be made to fail. It is always personal."[27] In this instance, what the fantasy frame helps to establish is the connection between political ideology and personal experience: by moving the focus from structural problems in the society to individual perceptions, personal examples trump statistical facts or logic. As seen through the Imaginary fantasy frame, political fictions take on the force of real perceptions.

In this context of political fantasies, it is also important to remember Freud's theories about how paranoia works: every detail or perception can be garnered to provide evidence for an already existing comprehensive interpretation.[28] With paranoid thinking, the conclusion comes first, and then the selected evidence is used to prove the already defined explanation. People then are picking not only their opinions but their facts, and so reason is used as an afterthought to strengthen an already determined insight. Moreover, the paranoid person is able to employ multiple and conflicting ideas in order to build up a conspiracy theory. For example, Frank shows how the Tea Party activists attacked the government's actions as the protesters both vilified and protected the banks: "For them, Democrats were devil figures; there was no contradiction in depicting them as both the pawns of the banks and also the persecutors of them. Democrats were so malignant they could play both roles simultaneously" (p. 59). What is then so hard for Frank and others to understand about this type of paranoid fantasy structure is the notion that facts do not really matter and the law of noncontradiction is suspended.

As Freud showed in his work on paranoia and jealousy, delusions are built out of the ability of the unconscious to use language in a way that reverses objects, subjects, and verbs.[29] Thus, instead of someone admitting that they hate something, they believe that someone else loves someone else. Paranoia is then an Imaginary use of unconscious thinking, which plays a central role in political ideology. Ultimately, what the paranoid person rejects and projects onto others is their own sense of guilt, shame, and desire. Freud added to this formation that the initial stage of psychosis concerns a withdrawal from the world, and the second stage represents an attempt to reconstruct the world on the level of an Imaginary delusion or fantasy.[30] In fact, Freud insists that while psychotics reconstruct the world through delusions, neurotics turn to the Imaginary realm of fantasy to reshape reality, and therefore, we can see how conservatives are not psychotic since they focus on the Imaginary interpretation of the world through the lens of the fantasy frame.

A key aspect of the paranoia on the Right can be found in Frank's discussion of the radio and television personality Glenn Beck: "[I]t was up to Beck to inform us that the government was crawling with secret subversives, that the president was building a private army, and that liberals were scheming to make the economy worse so that an anguished public would turn to them to fix things—the hard-times scenario as a left-wing doomsday device."[31] Beck here conforms to Freud's theory that the paranoid focuses on the secret actions of the persecutor in order to show that beneath appearances, one can find a secret plot that is not at first obvious.[32] In this structure, media pundits play an important role because they provide the interpretation to all of the hidden messages and secret plots.

Within a neoliberal context, conspiracy theories and political fantasies often emerge because people do not have systematic understanding of the complex social world around them. In the terms of Frederic Jameson, they lack "cognitive maps," and so in times of great change, they have to fabricate their own comprehensive interpretations through the combination of unconscious processes, Imaginary fantasies, social information, personal experience, and ideological prejudices.[33] As we see in Beck's discourse, part of the paranoid process involves ignoring certain things and exaggerating others: "'The end of America as you know it' was the modest way Glenn Beck described the health-care measure. Its object was 'robbing you of your humanity', protested Rush Limbaugh; another radio talker said it was 'the end of the Republic'."[34] Extremism thus begins with extreme interpretations organized by unconscious paranoid constructions,

or rather, paranoid political interpretations represent the conscious awareness of unconscious fantasies. As Freud argued throughout this work,
paranoid delusions are equivalent to neurotic fantasies and perverse performances, but what happens in truly psychotic delusions is that the
rejection (foreclosure) of internal ideas is perceived as an external perception coming from the Other.[35] In terms of paranoid delusions, the internal
conscience or superego is foreclosed, and one then feels that one is being
watched and the other knows one's thoughts. Freud argued that the
psychotic is actually correct here; the Other does know one's thoughts,
but the Other is one's internalized superego.

If we accept Freud's logic that in neurosis, reality is not foreclosed but it is
repressed and retained on the level of fantasy, what we find in paranoid
political rhetoric is the Imaginary idea that the government is the Other who
wants to invade our lives and regulate our freedom. These neurotic fantasies
also require a strict division of social groups into the categories of good and
evil, and Frank argues that we find these divisions highlighted throughout
Right-wing rhetoric: "America is made up of two classes, roughly speaking,
'ordinary people' and 'intellectuals'. According to this way of thinking, as we
see again and again, either you're a productive citizen, or you're some kind
of snob, a university professor or an EPA bureaucrat. Compared to the vivid
line separating intellectuals and productive members of society, all other
distinctions fade to nothingness. Between small-business owners and share-
croppers, for example, there is no difference at all ... "[36] Political manipulation then works by taking the paranoid need to oppose the good and the bad
and defining who is good and who is evil. In the case of the Tea Party
reaction to the financial crisis, the important move was to define the government and greedy homeowners as evil and not the banks. Likewise, the
conservative movement has focused on cultural elites and not the wealthy
as the people with power and control in society: "But for the conservatives
who had by then taken control of Congress, class is never about income or
wealth; it's about learning. Intellectuals are the villains at the top of the great
pyramid, just as they were during the years of the culture wars."[37] Like the
Nazi paranoid delusions concerning "the Jews" that Slavoj Zizek has
described so well, the intellectuals are blamed for the corruption of culture,
and this allows people to ignore the true source of power and conflict within
society.[38]

One reason why university professors, the media, and liberal politicians
are seen as the evil persecutors in Right-wing paranoid fantasies is that
these groups function as the externalized superego that watches over

people's thoughts and desires. Thus in the attack on political correctness, what is being defended against is often the Imaginary idea that the Left represents the social censor that monitors and condemns the thoughts and desires of the paranoid subject. In response to this repressive superego, the Right often likes politicians who appear to speak their mind and voice the prejudices that everyone wants to say but suppresses.

The paranoid fantasies of persecution also reinforce the notion that people on the Right are the real victims of society. Frank reveals this connection between persecution, paranoia, and victim identification in the following passage: "Stupid, backward, bigoted, racist. You've probably been called all this and more . . . Then one day, you had enough. You got tired of the attacks on private enterprise. [!] . . . Then you went to a tea party, and that's when you really crossed the line. Every morning the newspaper calls you a dangerous, hate-filled kook. Every night, the TV news declares you an ignorant, potentially violent redneck. And in between, political pundits and even politicians denounce you with juvenile insults like 'teabagger'."[39] The power of this type of Imaginary victim logic is that even when people are saying racist things, they feel that they are the ones being persecuted for speaking their minds. There is therefore no way to criticize the victim who is always seen as being innocent and pure and who is justified in any aggressive attack on others: "Depicting themselves as victimized in any and every situation is not merely a fun game of upside down; it is essential to their self-understanding. They are the ones to whom things are done. This is the reason they have taken as their banner a flag that reads, 'Don't Tread on Me'. The slogan is a concise expression of the grand distortion that undergirds everything I have been describing: the belief that we are living in an age of rampant leftism; that decades of unrelieved progressivism are what brought the nation to its awful straits; that markets were born free but are everywhere in chains."[40] Once again, Frank does an effective job at summarizing the rhetoric of the Right, but he is unable to explain how these distortions actually function because he does not have a psychoanalytic understanding of political fantasy.

We see some of the limitations of Frank's approach when he discusses one of the great promoters of reversed victimhood, which is Sarah Palin who was chosen to run for Vice President in 2008: "Even those who followed her career don't really know where Palin stood on many issues. We know only that she was constantly being maligned, that whenever we turned on the TV and saw her fair face beaming, we were about to hear that some liberal someone had slurred this noble lady yet again. Indeed, if political figures stand for ideas, victimization was what Sarah Palin was all about. It was her brand, her myth. But to become such a symbol, Palin had to do the opposite of most public figures: where others learn to take hostility in stride, she and her fans developed the thinnest of skins."[41] Although Frank wants to see this type of victim fantasy as a limited phenomenon, I have been arguing that it is actually one of the most powerful forces in politics today. For example, much of the rhetoric of the Christian Right is centered on the idea that abortion is a form of mass murder. What often brings this group together is that they identify with the victimized fetus, and this can be seen in the signs that they carry and the horror stories they repeat. Moreover, we find a similar victim identification in the representation of Jewish people as the victims of history. While we should not minimize the real suffering of Jews, we cannot ignore how this suffering has been used to justify the aggressive military actions of the state of Israel. In turn, Palestinians have responded to their mistreatment by Israel in affirming their own victim status and by attacking Israelis, and Arabs throughout the world have identified with this victimhood. Moreover, after the attacks of 9/11, the most powerful country in the world proclaimed its own innocent victim status. This chain of victim politics thus spreads throughout the globe and shapes the actions and reactions of many different political groups.[42]

Returning to Frank's discussion of the new American Right, he affirms the role victim identification plays in the conservative counterrevolution: "Understanding themselves as the true victims is, in fact, essential to the conservative revival. There are few political or cultural situations in which they don't instinctively reach for the mantle of the wronged, holler about bias, or protest about how unfairly they've been treated."[43] The Right then unifies around their victim status as they attack other social groups for claiming to be victims of discrimination or poverty. In the constant-sum game of victim competition, only one political group can be the victim, and everyone else must be a persecutor. For example, in turning to Ayn Rand's influential book *Atlas Shrugged*, Frank shows how this writer helped to provide victim identification material for the new Right: "As per the genre's requirements, its protagonists are noble producers who are unfairly oppressed. But in this iteration of the proletarian novel, the self-interested businessman is the hero instead of the villain. The parasites are the rest of us, the rabble and the intellectuals who use government to mooch and freeload on the labors of the virtuous capitalist."[44] In this upside-down world of Right-wing victim politics, the wealthy capitalists are the victims, while the poor people needing government assistance are the victimizers.

This neoliberal conservative logic was exported throughout the world with the World Bank and the International Monetary Fund, which used aid to poor countries as a way of forcing them to open up their markets to global penetration while requiring that they agree to cut their public services and privatize their national industries.[45] Under the banner of "structural adjustment," liberals and conservatives colluded to represent the wealthy elites of Third World countries as the victims of excessive government spending and the poor as the victimizers. To fix this situation, the victims had to be victimized and the victimizers had to be set free.

In the context of the United States, much has been written on how this counterrevolution was organized to wrest political power from liberal democrats and to allow for the reduction of taxes through the defunding and debasement of Big Government.[46] According to this narrative, wealthy business people organized to form think tanks and fund elections in order to convince fellow citizens that taxes were a form of theft and government regulation was stopping prosperity. This same group used coded racism in order to turn working class whites against the Democratic Party and help divide the working class. Yet, none of these political manipulations would have worked if they were not focused on manipulating Imaginary fantasies and identifications. Therefore, it is hard to understand the Right if we do not mobilize psychoanalytic theories and practices.

In the case of Ayn Rand, her political victim fantasies were able to strike a chord with individuals who experienced themselves as victims no matter their power or their wealth: "Captains of industry are 'the great victims,' as one character puts it, 'who have contributed the most and suffered the worst injustice in return'. And as the long, long novel plods slowly on, Rand doubles down on the idea, having John Galt declare himself to be 'the defender of the oppressed, the disinherited, the exploited–and when I use those words, they have, for once, a literal meaning'."[47] Just as Freud argues in "A Child is Being Beaten" that the sources of masochistic and sadistic fantasies often come from literary texts, Frank shows how the Right was able to use Rand's novel to construct a fantasy world where wealthy business people are the real victims, and poor workers are the victimizers.[48]

Rand is known as one of the key figures of the Libertarian Right, and Frank highlights what connects her work to Libertarians like Frederick Hayek and Ludwig von Mises is a shared paranoid fantasy of victim reversal: "The libertarian economist Ludwig von Mises loved *Atlas Shrugged*, nailing the book's antipopulist message in a single perceptive sentence. 'You have the courage to tell the masses what no politician told them', he wrote in a fan letter to Rand: 'you are inferior and all the improvements in your conditions which you simply take for granted you owe to the efforts of men who are better than you'."[49] This famous Austrian economist was perhaps saying something that one is not supposed to say in public, which is that behind the false populism of the Right, we can find a strong antipopulist message: the people should realize that everything they get comes from the incredible superiority of the wealthy corporate tycoons, but the fearful politicians are afraid to tell the people that they are the real losers.

This attack on the people on behalf of the people reaches its climatic apex in a scene that Frank describes from Rand's novel: "And then, in a notorious passage, the narrator goes through all the other passenger cars on the train and tells us why each casualty-to-be deserves the fate that is coming to him or her. One of them, she points out, received government loans; another doesn't like businessmen; a third is married to a federal regulator; a fourth foolishly thinks she has a right to ride on a train even when she doesn't personally own the train in question. For each one of these subhumans, the sentence is death."[50] Although it should be clear why wealthy business people may not like government loans and federal regulators, it remains unclear for Frank why working class people would identify with this discourse.

To help explain this self-defeating political identification, Frank turns toward to a nonpsychoanalytic understanding: "But more disturbingly, there is a certain remoteness from reality, a kind of politicized groupthink that seems to get worse each year as the Right withdraws ever farther into a world of its own."[51] The problem with this explanation is that it really does not explain much: what is needed is the connection between masochistic victim fantasies and the identification with the aggressor. In fact, as Freud argues in his theory of masochism, the humiliated subject identifies with the one doing the humiliation.[52] Furthermore, people identify with the narcissism of the other because they see this as the only way they can recapture their own lost power and enjoyment.[53] Freud's theory of secondary narcissism, therefore, helps us to understand why people will not only pity the billionaire, but they will also make sure that the billionaire does not have to deal with taxes or government regulations. Due to Imaginary identifications, disempowered people are able to identify with the wealth and power of the rich. Once again, it is hard to understand this political structure, if one does not have a notion of the way Imaginary consciousness allows for identification to replace desire as reality is combined with fiction and pain becomes pleasure.

HYSTORIES

Related to the psychoanalytic notions of masochism, Imaginary victim-hood, and identification, we find the role played by the media in circulating cultural material that can be used in the formation of fantasy structures. As Elaine Showalter claimed in her book *Hystories*, hysterical patients have always constructed their fantasies and symptoms out of surrounding social content.[54] For instance, she depicts how fantasies regarding alien abductions and satanic abuse rituals have a clear cultural source, but they also are experienced in a highly personal way. Like stories of sacrifice and humiliation, cultural media have always fed into victim fantasies, but as Frank insists, what we are witnessing now is a massive increase in the production and polarization of political discourse in the media: "Conservatives inhabit a 'very separate world', declared the Democratic pollster Stanley Greenberg in 2009; a place of intense group identity where Fox News is the medium of record and the president is believed to follow a 'secret agenda' that is invisible to the rest of the nation. This culture of closure also gives us the phrase 'Don't Believe the Liberal Media'—the slogan of the Media Research Center, an important player in winger Washington."[55] Since hysterics identify with the suffering of others and paranoid people believe in secret plots, we can see how the media feeds into these pathologies by providing the material for cultural and personal fantasies.

Frank highlights that one of the things that allows the Right to utilize this hysterical paranoid rhetoric is that the Left has failed to come up with their own responses and interpretations: "From its silver-tongued leader on down, Democrats simply could not tell us why our system had run aground and why we had a stake in doing things differently. They could not summon an ideology of their own."[56] As many political scientists and progressive critics have argued, when the Left does not provide an effective set of policies and explanations, then people turn to the populist Right.[57] In fact, Frank insists that it is because the Democrats are also invested in the smooth running of the current political and capitalist machine that they cannot present a real alternative, which would challenge the discourse and fantasies of the Right: "It is easy to understand how Democrats evolved into this tongue-tied, expert-worshipping species. Their traditional Democratic solutions may well have solved our problems, as Christina Romer maintained, but the ideology behind those solutions— as well as the solutions themselves, in many cases–are totally unacceptable to the people who increasingly fund Democratic campaigns."[58] Since Democrats have also bought into the system that forces politicians to spend much of their time raising money for campaigns from powerful, wealthy donors, they have little ability to provide a different set of political explanations.

Exploring Unconscious Racism

In Chapter 3, I will provide a psychoanalytic explanation of why the liberal Left has been unable to present an alternative political agenda. However, before I move on from this examination of the Right, it is important to examine the role that racism has played in the current counterrevolution. The first reason this is necessary is because for the last 40 years, the Right has been using an indirect, coded form of racism that helps to solidify its base through the communication of unconscious messages. As Michelle Alexander explains in *The New Jim Crow*, Republicans who sought to win the South from the Democrats after the passage of Civil Rights legislation in 1964 realized that they could no longer use explicit racism to attract white voters.[59] Instead, the Right had to find indirect ways to win over people, and one of the first strategies they developed was to use crime as a code word for blacks. Politicians like Richard Nixon in his Southern Strategy realized that if they talked about getting tough on crime, white voters would on an unconscious level associate criminal behavior with black people. Not only did this trick help to activate *and* hide racist feelings, but it also opened up the door for a form of political discourse based on unconscious associations and conscious disavowal. In this structure, people could deny their own racism at the same time they were acting on racist prejudices. In what is now called "dog whistle" politics, politicians have unconsciously keyed into the unconscious through the use of displaced symbolism and affect, and we see a clear example of this type of unconscious communication through the representation of "the immigrant" as a code for the racial and cultural other.[60] Unconscious racism helps to bring together victim identification and the primary fantasy of total freedom and enjoyment by arguing that it is the hated Other who is victimizing us and preventing our nation from being free and unified.

The use of victim identification, unconscious racism, and the fantasy of total freedom helps us to explain the foundations of the conservative coalition in the United States and around the world. One of the great mysteries of this political formation is the ability since the neoliberal age of Reagan to unify free market capitalists, racist nationalists, civil liberty libertarians, and Christian fundamentalists to work together and to support the same candidates. On one level, there should be a strong conflict between Christians and libertarians: after all, Christians want the government to enforce laws against abortion and gay marriage, and much of Christ's discourse is a criticism of the focus on money and wealth. Moreover, how can Christians support the hatred of racist nationalists, and why would nationalists support the free market policies of global capitalism? In turn, the civil liberty libertarians should be against the promotion of the military by the nationalists and the Christian push for governmental restrictions concerning private matters (abortion, marriage). What I have been arguing is that what really holds this contradictory coalition together is two Imaginary fantasies united in a symptomatic mode of identification. While the civil liberty and free market libertarians unite over the fantasy of total freedom and enjoyment, the Christian fundamentalists and the racist nationalists bond over the fantasy of victimhood. In turn, these two opposing fantasy structures are united in the symptom, which according to Freud always combines together two contrasting fantasies.

NOTES

1. I focus on the work of Freud and Lacan because I believe they offer the most comprehensive and effective system for understanding psychoanalysis. Other analysts and theorists have made important contributions to the field, but only Freud and Lacan approach analysis through an integrated system of the key concepts.
2. Lacan, J. (2001). The mirror stage as formative of the function of the I. In *Ecrits: A selection* (trans: Sheridan, A.) (pp. 1–8). New York: Norton.
3. Although Slavoj Zizek is one of the most recognized contemporary psychoanalytic critics of politics and fantasy, I argue that his theory suffers from his neglect of the role played by the Imaginary in psychoanalysis and politics.
4. For an extensive analysis of victim politics in American society, see Cole, A.M. (2007). *The cult of true victimhood: From the War on welfare to the War on Terror*. Palo Alto: Stanford University Press.
5. Thomas, F. (2012). *Pity the billionaire: The hard-times swindle and the unlikely comeback of the right*. New York: Macmillan, p. 7.

6. For in-depth analysis of the history of the politics of victim identification, see *The Cult of True Victimhood*.
7. For a discussion and criticism of Freud's development of his theory of victim see fantasies, see Clark, R.W. (1980). *Freud: The man and the cause*. Jonathan Cape, p. 156; Garcia, E.E. (1987). Freud's seduction theory. *The Psychological Study of the* Schimek, J.G. (1987). Fact and fantasy in the seduction theory: A historical review. *Journal of the American Psychoanalytic Association, xxxv*, 937–965; Israëls, H., & Schatzman, M. (1993). The seduction theory. *History of Psychiatry, iv*, 23–59; McCullough, M.L. (2001). Freud's seduction theory and its rehabilitation: A saga of one mistake after another. *Review of General Psychology, 5*(1), 3–22.
8. Breuer, J., Freud, S., & Strachey, J. (2000). *Studies on hysteria*. New York: Basic Books.
9. Lacan, J., & Mitchell, J. (1985). *Feminine sexuality: Jacques Lacan and the Ecole Freudienne*. New York: WW Norton & Company.
10. Freud, S. (1975). *Group psychology and the analysis of the ego*. New York: WW Norton & Company, p. 49.
11. Frank, *Pity*, p. 10.
12. Freud, S. (1959). Hysterical phantasies and their relation to bisexuality. In *The standard edition of the complete psychological works of Sigmund Freud, Volume IX (1906–1908): Jensen's 'Gradiva' and other works* (pp. 155–166). London: Hogarth.
13. Freud, S. (1963). *Civilization and its discontents*. New York: Norton, p. 13.
14. Freud, S. (1997). *General psychological theory: Papers on metapsychology*. New York: Simon and Schuster, p. 27.
15. Freud, S. (1958). Formulations on the two principles of mental functioning. In *The standard edition of the complete psychological works of Sigmund Freud, Volume XII (1911–1913): The case of Schreber, papers on technique and other works* (pp. 213–226). London: Hogarth.
16. Freud, S., (1920). *Totem and Taboo: Resemblances between the psychic lives of savages and neurotics*. New York: Norton.
17. Ibid., pp. 207–209.
18. Frank, *Pity*, p. 11.
19. Ibid., p. 28.
20. For the break with nature in human sexuality, see Lacan's deconstruction of the drive in Lacan, J. (1977). *Four fundamental concepts of psychoanalysis*. New York: Norton, pp. 161–173.
21. Frank, *Pity*, p. 45.
22. Cole, *The Cult*, p. 5.
23. Ibid., pp. 2–4.
24. Ibid., p. 4.
25. Frank, *Pity*, p. 49.

26. Laclau, E., (2005). *On populist reason*. London: Verso, p. 94.
27. Frank, *Pity*, p. 53.
28. Freud, S. (1922). Some neurotic mechanisms in jealousy, paranoia and homosexuality. In *Standard edition* (Vol. 18, pp. 221–232). London: Hogarth.
29. Ibid.
30. Freud, S. (1997). *General psychological theory: Papers on metapsychology* (Vol. 6). New York: Simon and Schuster, p. 41.
31. Frank, *Pity*, p. 64.
32. Freud, S. (2001). *An infantile neurosis*. New York: Random House.
33. Jameson, F. (1991). *Postmodernism, or, the cultural logic of late capitalism*. Raleigh: Duke University Press.
34. Frank, *Pity*, p. 66.
35. Freud, S. (2014). *Psycho-Analytic notes on an autobiographical account of a case of paranoia (dementia paranoides)*. New York: Read Books Ltd.
36. Frank, *Pity*, p. 96.
37. Ibid., p. 94.
38. Žižek, S. (1989). *The sublime object of ideology*. London: Verso, pp. 48–49, 125, 176.
39. Frank, *Pity*, p. 127.
40. Ibid., p. 128.
41. Ibid.
42. I analyze these dynamics throughout, Samuels, R. (2007). *Teaching the rhetoric of resistance: The popular holocaust and social change in a post 9/11 World*. New York: Macmillan.
43. Frank, *Pity*, p. 129.
44. Ibid, p. 149.
45. Stiglitz, J.E. (2002). *Globalization and its discontents*. Norton: New York; Klein, N. (2007). *The shock doctrine: The rise of disaster capitalism*. New York: Macmillan.
46. Krugman, P. (2009) *The conscience of a liberal*. New York: WW Norton & Company; Huffington, A. (2011). *Third World America: How our politicians are abandoning the middle class and betraying the American dream*. New York: Broadway Books; Brown, W. (2006). American nightmare neoliberalism, neoconservatism, and de-democratization. *Political theory, 34*(6), 690–714.
47. Frank, *Pity*, p. 150.
48. Freud, S. (1922). A child is being beaten. *The Journal of Nervous and Mental Disease, 56*(4), 405–406.
49. Frank, *Pity*, p. 150.
50. Ibid., 151.
51. Ibid., 158.

52. Freud, S. (1929). The economic problem of masochism. In *The psychoanalytic review (1913–1957)*, pp. *16*, 209.
53. Freud, S. (2014). *On Narcissism: An introduction*. New York: Read Books Ltd.
54. Showalter, E. (1998). *Hystories: Hysterical epidemics and modern media*. New York: Columbia University Press.
55. Frank, *Pity*, p. 159.
56. Ibid., p. 174.
57. Hedges, C. (2011). *Death of the liberal Class*. New York: Vintage Books.
58. Frank, *Pity*, p. 174.
59. Alexander, M. (2012). *The new Jim Crow: Mass incarceration in the age of colorblindness*. New York: The New Press.
60. For more on unconscious racism, see Vedantam, S. (2010). *The hidden brain: How our unconscious minds elect presidents, control markets, Wage Wars, and save our lives*. New York: Random House Digital, Inc.

CHAPTER 3

Beyond Hillary Clinton: Obsessional Narcissism and the Failure of the Liberal Class

Abstract This chapter turns to a psychoanalytic understanding of the liberal aspects of neoliberal politics. Using Freud's theories of transference, narcissism, and obsessional neurosis, I posit that liberals often want to deny their own aggression by having their ideal self-recognized by an ideal other, and so they often cling to a rhetoric of progressive moral righteousness as they engage in destructive acts of competitive capitalism. I explore how progressive social movements can avoid the pitfalls of narcissistic transference by creating political organizations that move beyond identification, idealization, and cynical conformity.

Keywords Liberal · Thomas Frank · Obsessional narcissism · Hillary Clinton · Meritocracy · Transference · Narcissism · Higher education · Working class · Idealization · Freud · Lacan

To understand the reasons why the American Left has failed to provide an effective counter to the Right, we must examine how the psychopathology of meritocratic narcissism rules the liberal class. Throughout this work, I will define this cultural pathology by several key elements: (1) an overinvestment in seeing the self as good and well intentioned: (2) a belief that we have a fair meritocratic system that rewards talent and intelligence; (3) a fear of criticism, conflict, and aggression; and (4) a narcissistic investment in idealizing

© The Author(s) 2016

R. Samuels, *Psychoanalyzing the Left and Right After Donald Trump,*
Critical Theory and Practice in Psychology and the Human Sciences,
DOI 10.1007/978-3-319-44808-4_3

others. As in the case of narcissistic personality disorders, liberals often need others to see them as well intentioned because they define themselves by how others see them. To understand this structure, we have to return to Freud's early insights into transference where he discovered that people will censor themselves in psychoanalysis because they are afraid of what other people think about their desires and aggression. Thus, what often blocks free association and the process of psychoanalysis is the way that patients place the analyst in the position of the ego ideal, which Lacan argues is the place where people see themselves as loveable.[1] However, for psychoanalytic treatment to work, the patient has to say whatever is on his or her mind without worrying what the analyst thinks; Freud called this process free association because the speaker is supposed to be free from self-censorship. For Lacan, Symbolic speech transcends the Imaginary relationship between the ego and the other, but we shall see that this move toward social mediation is blocked when one identifies with the ego ideal as the source of self-censorship and the verification of the ideal ego. In the case of many liberals, they want to be idealized by ideal others, and this entails conforming to an idealized meritocratic social system as they enact performances of conspicuous progressive morality.

One might ask what is wrong with people trying to conform to a meritocracy? After all, isn't a meritocracy better than an aristocracy? The answer to these questions centers on the fact that we really do not have a fair meritocracy in a system where 80 % of all wealth is the direct and indirect result of inheritance.[2] We also do not have a fair system when standardized college test (SAT) scores are correlated with wealth, and college rankings and admissions are determined largely by these scores.[3] In our highly unequal society, the liberal solution to inequality and poverty is usually education, and yet education often enhances inequality in our meritocracy.[4] Ultimately, by producing and maintaining the failed meritocracy, neoliberal liberals end up supporting inequality and poverty, but they cannot recognize this connection because they are so invested in seeing themselves as doing good, and they reject any criticism that would shatter their idealized self-image. Fundamentally, meritocratic narcissism is based on the desire to engage in competitive capitalism without having to feel any guilt for the losers of the system.

On a global scale, we find the spread of this American model of neoliberal subjectivity through failed aid and charitable interventions. In pushing an agenda that education is the key to eradicating global poverty and inequality, we have witnessed the inability to challenge the concentration of wealth and power in "poor" nations. Moreover, the failures of these development policies have been repressed by the desire of the benefactors to see their actions as only leading to good.[5] To make things worse, the use of foreign experts to determine economic and political strategies for "developing" nations often results in the liberal experts failing to understand the actual needs of the people on the ground as money is funneled to the elites of the society.

Of course there is a danger in making such broad generalizations about a large group of people, and yet it is important to look at general social tendencies in order to see how political affiliations are determined by conscious and unconscious motivations. Thus, in the last chapter, I examined how the conservative counterrevolution is dominated by the Imaginary fantasies of unlimited power, victim identification, paranoid thinking, and indirect racism. This combination of social and psychological formations serves to deny the fact that capitalism is a system that generates inequality, poverty, instability, and a lack of social trust. In the case of liberals, many of the destructive aspects of capitalism are hidden by the narcissistic investment in the ideology of a fair meritocracy. Moreover, just as conservative politicians often unify their coalition over a shared hatred of liberals, liberals coalesce over their fear of conservatives and radical alternatives. Political polarization therefore helps to unify both liberals and conservatives as each group refuses to deal with the destructive aspects of contemporary neoliberal capitalism.

In describing liberals and conservatives from a social and psychoanalytic perspective, I am focusing on ideal types and not on the many different variations we can find in society. Just as no one is purely obsessional or sadistic, not all conservatives are paranoid hysterics and not all liberals are obsessional narcissists; however, it is still productive to use these categories to organize a wide range of behaviors under a single type. In fact, as our society continues to sort itself into more polarized cultural groups, the power of these ideal types only continues to grow. Furthermore, it is my argument that psychoanalytic theory often provides the key missing link to understanding how these political ideologies are produced and maintained.

OBSESSIONAL NARCISSISM

In order to help explain the psychopathology behind contemporary liberalism, I have developed the concept of obsessional narcissism. This theory combines both Freud's initial insights about narcissism and obsessional neurosis with the recent American psychoanalytic argument that most patients today are not neurotic because they are better described as suffering from narcissistic personality disorders.[6] From the contemporary American psychoanalytic and psychotherapeutic perspective, Freud is no longer very useful because narcissistic personalities do not respond well to analysis. My argument is that most people who are currently diagnosed as being narcissistic are very similar to what Freud called obsessive-compulsive neurotics, and this means that Freud's initial theories are still valid but can also be enhanced by looking at current social and cultural changes.

The starting point to understand Freud's take on obsessional narcissism is the case of the Rat Man.[7] Early on his discussion of his treatment of this man, Freud relates that when he asked the patient why he spent so much time discussing his early sexual experiences, the patient replied that he knew of Freud's theories.[8] Like a good student who gives back to the teacher on exams what he thinks the teacher believes and knows, the Rat Man shows how in the transference relationship, the patient tries to anticipate the understanding of the analyst. As any psychoanalyst knows who has worked with obsessional narcissistic patients, it is very hard to get them to free associate because they are so concerned about what the analyst is thinking about them.[9] Just as the Rat Man was saying to Freud what he thought Freud wanted to hear, obsessional narcissistic patients want to control the flow of discourse by conforming to the knowledge of the other and censoring themselves. This act of self-censorship is the central resistance to free association and hinders the goals of psychoanalysis itself; moreover, we shall see that self-censoring plays a key role in the development of neoliberal subjectivity.

In his later writings on psychoanalytic work, Freud will point out that whenever the patient suddenly stops free associating, you can be sure that he/she is thinking about the presence of the analyst.[10] In this case, we see that transference represents self-censorship and the obstacle to free association. Yet, transference also represents a necessary part of analysis. In fact, Freud mentions that the Rat Man decided to come see Freud because he thought that some of Freud's written explanations reminded him of his own ideas.[11] The positive transference thus began before the analysis and was based on the idea that the analyst knows the patient's thoughts. As Lacan will later write, transference is centered on the illusion of the analyst being placed in the position of the one who is supposed to know.[12]

Transference therefore is dependent on an idealization of knowledge and the one who knows, and here we see the first connection to the neoliberal meritocracy, which is also based on idealizing knowledge and the people who have been certified as the ones who know. In fact, Freud begins his case study of the Rat Man by pointing out that this patient had a university education and that before this patient came to analysis, he would tell his problems to a friend of whom he had "an extraordinarily high opinion."[13] We can see that the transference with Freud began before they met, and Freud represented a substitute for a friend who was highly empathic: "His friend used then to give him moral support by assuring him that he was a man of irreproachable conduct..."[14] Like most obsessional narcissistic patients, the Rat Man wanted Freud and his friends to verify his good intentions; in other words, he was looking for an ego ideal who would support his ideal ego.[15]

Meritocratic narcissism can therefore be understood as an essential part of a social system that idealizes knowledge and talent and serves to make people feel that they are worthy and good. As a way of reinforcing the idealization of the self, meritocracy is a social structure that appears to focus on the isolated individual, but the truth is that the individual is defined purely in relation to others. As Lacan shows, in Imaginary narcissism, others are treated as mirror reflections or people who verify the subject's own idealized self. Likewise, Heinz Kohut argued that with narcissistic patients, one finds a mirroring or an idealizing transference.[16] However, while Kohut thought the role of the analyst was to support mirroring and idealization, Lacan argued that these narcissistic transferences are exactly what block the effectiveness of analysis. What Lacan warned against was the notion that the analyst should be idealized by the patient as the one who knows.[17] In fact, Freud also warned against the analyst taking on this position of idealized knowledge: "If the patient puts the analyst in the position of the father (or mother), he is also giving him the power which his super-ego exercises over his ego... But at this point a warning must be given against misusing the new influence. However much the analyst may be tempted to become a teacher, model and ideal for other people and to create men in his own image, he should not forget that this is not his task in the analytic relationship, and indeed that he will be indeed disloyal to his task if he allows himself to be led on by his inclinations. If he does, he will only be repeating a mistake of the parents who crushed their child's independence by their influence, and he only will be replacing the patent's earlier dependence by a new one."[18] This passage is key to understanding Freud's analytic method: since he was dedicated to preserving the independence of his patients, he realized that the analyst could not be an ideal or a model for them. He also contrasted psychoanalysis with education and warned the analyst against being a teacher. Here is where we find a clear critique of meritocratic narcissism: the analytic process suspends the Imaginary transference that places the Other in the position of the ego ideal or superego.

Although we often think of neoliberalism as a conservative political movement based on the privatization of public institutions, the downsizing of the welfare state, and the celebration of the deregulated free market, there is also a liberal form of neoliberalism centered on the educational meritocracy and the rejection of any real alternatives to the current capitalist system. Thus, instead of trying to fight poverty and inequality, the liberal class turns toward education as the central mechanism to revolve economic and social problems. However, in the face of evidence that education actually increases inequality and decreases social mobility, the liberal class represses this failure of the meritocracy and focuses on making sure that their own children outcompete others in the meritocratic race. As Freud argued in relation to narcissism, parents see their child as an idealized representation of their own lost narcissism, and so the educational success of the child represents proof of the parents' own ability to attain the cultural ideal.[19]

A great example of how obsessional narcissism works in our current culture is the web site Facebook, which allows people to post pictures and descriptions of their lives or interesting current events, and the only option given to the audience at first was to push a "like" button. Here we see how the externalized self (the ideal ego) is verified by the ideal Other (the ego ideal). In this structure, what the narcissist does not want is to have his or her self-image rejected or criticized. For both Lacan and Kohut, this need for the Other to approve of the narcissistic self stems from the way that parents affirm or reject the child's displays of grandiosity. Kohut argues that if the parent does not recognize the child, the child will continually seek recognition throughout life. However, if a parent does nothing but applaud the child's exhibitionism, the child will also seek approval in an obsessional way. Kohut insists that the parent must maintain the optimal level of frustration and recognition.[20]

For Lacan, one of the central tasks of the analyst is to handle the patient's demand for recognition and understanding. Although the analyst is trained not to respond to the demands of the patient, a lack of response can produce so much anxiety that the analysis no longer functions. The analyst then must find a way to both not feed the narcissistic transference and not allow for too much anxiety to emerge. For Lacan, the main method for handling the demands of the patients for the analyst to be the one who knows is through interpretation. However, instead of seeing interpretation as the analyst providing meaning and new knowledge for the patient, analytic interpretation must aim to open up more free associations.[21] The main function of the analyst is therefore to promote free association and to suspend the demands for satisfaction, idealization, and identification.

One of Lacan's main innovations in how to handle the transference and allow for free association was his method for the ending of each session. Instead of submitting to the predetermined, ritualistic 50-minute hour, the Lacanian analyst ends sessions when free association is no longer working or when there is too much anxiety or to highlight an important moment in analysis. During my own Lacanian analysis, my experience was that because I did not know when the session would end, I tried to speak as fast as I could, and this helped me to overcome my resistance to free association. In fact, I would argue that one of the main things one can gain from analysis is the ability to speak in public about anything without fear.[22]

It is interesting to note that in our current neoliberal meritocracy, many professionals today claim that their biggest fear and what causes the most anxiety is public speaking. This fear is in part derived from the narcissistic desire to not look bad in front of others. As my students often tell me, they do not want to look too stupid or too smart in class discussions, so they tend to say nothing. From a psychoanalytic perspective, we know that this fear of speaking is derived from the fear of being criticized by not only the external Other but also the internalized superego. After all, Freud argued that the superego judges the ego in relationship to the ego ideal.[23] Since the ideals of the ego are derived from society, we can see how meritocracy links up to narcissism: in a meritocratic system, one is judged by how well one conforms to the ideals of the culture, and the failure to live up to the judgments of others results in a loss of self-esteem.

In the case of liberal and progressive politics, the obsessional narcissist wants to be recognized by others for how he or she is conforming to the ideals of the culture, and to gain this recognition, it is necessary to intentionally perform explicit acts of goodness. Yet, as Freud argues in the Rat Man case, "the moral self was the conscious, the evil self was the unconscious."[24] In other words, when people express good intentions, they may be trying to repress hostile impulses. For example, since narcissists want to be recognized for their intelligence and moral goodness, they cannot tolerate any criticism that reveals their "sinful" unconscious desires or their failure to conform to the cultural ideal. In fact, after Freud explains this idea to the Rat Man, the patient reacts with doubt and hostility, and Freud responds in the following way: "I said a word or two upon the good opinion I had formed of him, and this gave him visible pleasure."[25] It should be clear here that Freud did not yet figure out how to handle the narcissistic transference and the desire of the patient to be idealized by the analyst.

However, one of the important things about Freud is that he was not afraid to reveal the limits of his knowledge. For example, in the introduction to this case, he admits that he is only offering incomplete "crumbs of knowledge," which may not be satisfying in themselves but open up the door for future research by other investigators.[26] This acknowledgement of the limits of knowledge represents the inverse of the transference where the subject wants to believe that the Other is all knowing. As Freud will later discover, the key to analysis is to realize that someone will only fully accept knowledge if it comes from their own thinking and being, and therefore, the analyst cannot play the role of the savior or sage.

THE CULTURE OF MERITOCRATIC NARCISSISM

This critique of the one who knows flies in the face of our current meritocracy that is often centered on seeing education as the testing place that certifies who does and does not know. As Thomas Frank argues in his *Listen, Liberal*, the liberal class is now dominated by an educational elite of experts who believe that they are the ones who know. For instance, in the case of charity and development aid, we find that the discourse of good intentions often produces negative results, but few people want to acknowledge the failure of their projects dedicated to helping others.[27] In many ways, we are blinded by our good intentions, and as Lacan argues, beneath every act of charity, we can often find hidden aggression.[28] Not only do people want to feel good about themselves by showing how they are helping others, but they often unconsciously look down on the people they are aiding.

A key then to understanding the pathology of liberalism is to understand that public displays of good intentions may be harboring unconscious hostility. Moreover, it is hard to point out the shortcoming of these intentions and actions because the need to be seen as good serves to reject any criticism of the self. Ultimately, in our age of global capitalism, it is the destructive nature of greed and short-term self-interest that is often veiled by good intentions. For example, in higher education, there are many liberal professors who present themselves as being morally progressive by promoting diversity and human rights, yet they are also highly concerned about their own careers and their need to be part of elite institutions. The result of this combined investment in progressive ideals and competitive careerism is that they often repress their role in maintaining an exploitive labor system and an anti-democratic admissions structure.[29]

As a faculty union president, I have had the opportunity to work with many "liberal" professors who become quite aggressive when they are confronted with the reality of the exploitive labor system that supports their work. Since progressive faculty want to believe that they are good people doing good work, they do not want to deal with issues like the exploitation of part-time faculty and graduate students. They also often do not want to confront the use of SAT scores in college admissions, which reward wealthy students with merit scholarships and access to elite institutions. Moreover, even when liberal professors and institutions question the value of college ranking systems, each school tries to outcompete other schools in order to become the most elite. In turn, elite liberal professors rely on college rankings in order to verify their status and compete in the market for better pay and more prestige. These faculty members are torn between their need to see themselves as being part of a morally good enterprise and their desire to outcompete others in the meritocratic race.

According to Frank, it is this narcissistic investment in the higher education meritocracy that is one of the main causes for the failure of the liberal class to confront issues of labor and inequality. Since liberal politicians believe that the best way for people to get ahead in society and improve the economy is through higher education, they do not look at how higher education actually enhances inequality and decreases social mobility.[30] They also tend to not focus on the other main causes of poverty, such as the loss of unions, the use of part-time workers, and the globalization of labor. Since the liberal class avoids seeking radical alternatives to the current economic systems as it avoids helping the working class, the Right is able to attract disaffected workers and create an alliance between wealthy elites and the victims of neoliberal capitalist globalization.

THE POVERTY OF LIBERALISM

Since liberals at the top of the social system are often successful products of the meritocracy, they believe that the system works and is fair; however, as Frank attests, this belief can only be sustained if they turn their back on workers and the middle class: "When it comes to tackling the 'defining challenge of our time', however, many of our modern Democratic leaders falter. They acknowledge that inequality is rampant and awful, but they cannot find the conviction or imagination to do what is necessary to reverse it. Instead they offer the same high-minded demurrals and policy platitudes they've been offering since the 1980s. They remind us that there's nothing anyone can do about globalization or technology. They promise charter schools, and job training, and student loans, but other than that—well, they've got nothing."[31] Frank argues here that Democrats have had a hard time dealing with inequality as they often see education as the solution to every economic problem. From this perspective, liberals are blinded by their investment in the meritocracy, but what Frank does not fully examine is: How can they still feel good about themselves and their policies when they in fact have the effect of increasing inequality and poverty?

From a psychoanalytic perspective, we have seen that the theory of obsessional narcissism can aid us in our effort to understand why well-intentioned people are blind to the destructive effects of their actions. On one level, there is the fear of criticism and the need to be seen by ideal others as being morally good. However, on a deeper level, there is the unconscious hostility toward others that has to be constantly repressed in order to preserve a positive self-image. It turns out that liberals not only want to promote a more just world, but they also want to outcompete others in the capitalist contest for social power. Neoliberal liberalism then is structured by a contradiction that combines together democratic equality and capitalist competition; according to this ideology, everyone should have an equal opportunity to outcompete everyone else. Yet, the problem with this system is that the winners of the contest continually rewrite the rules so that they guarantee that they will continue to win, while they help to produce a class of losers, who often become the targets of their unconscious scorn.

We can consider that the underlying pathology of liberal obsessional narcissism is a sense of guilt that has to be constantly shouted down by acts of conspicuous moral righteousness. Since liberals know at some level that they are part of a destructive system, but they still want to outcompete others in the system, they have to repress their guilt and replace it with evidence of their goodness. For example, liberals like to display their morality by driving hybrid cars and carrying organic shopping bags that show their concern for the environment.[32] Likewise, large corporations like to advertise how diverse they are and how "green" they have become. Not only do these companies want to attract customers who desire to combine consumerism with political activism, but these companies also want to hide their own guilt behind a veil of goodness.

Of course, one could say that I am simply following the Right who attacks liberals for being hypocritical in their explicit acts of goodness.[33] However, it is important to stress that while the Right only sees hypocrisy, I see contradictions and unconscious motivations. Following Frank, this analysis seeks to answer the question of why has the liberal class failed to confront poverty and inequality: "What ails the Democrats? So bravely forthright on cultural issues, their leaders fold when confronted with matters of basic economic democracy. Why? What is it about this set of issues that transforms Democrats into vacillating softies, convinced that the big social question is beyond their control?"[34] For Chris Hedges in his *Death of the Liberal Class*, the answer is clear: liberals have sold out by focusing on their own careers and turning universities, unions, media outlets, and the Democratic Party into mechanisms for personal advancement. Even though, I also argue that this focus on personal gain is a big part of the problem, we also need to return to the psychoanalytic concept of obsessional narcissism to explain what allows people the ability to disregard how their actions contribute to the problems they bemoan.

For Frank, one major reason why the Democratic Party has been corrupted is the role that money plays in funding political campaigns: "The standard explanation is money and the way it runs through politics, adjusting incentives and distorting priorities wherever it flows. The country's leaders, this theory goes, are the products of a corrupt campaign finance system, their values whacked by the revolving door between Congress and K Street, between the Treasury Department and the banks. While parts of the oligarchy that rules this land and funds our politicians might not really object to something like gay marriage, when it comes to putting big banks into receivership—oh, no."[35] Clearly, as Bernie Sanders has stressed, we have a corrupt political system that allows wealthy people and large corporations to influence politicians and legislation; moreover, liberals like Hillary Clinton are often seen as products of a political system that has been manipulated by powerful interest groups, and so many people do not believe that she is honest or trustworthy. Even when Clinton critiques the campaign finance system, people see that she is still profiting from it, and so public trust is undermined.

Frank returns to the meritocracy to explain why liberals like Clinton buy into this system: "To diagnose their particular malady we must understand that there are different hierarchies of power in America, and while oligarchy theory exposes one of them—the hierarchy of money—many of the Democrats' failings arise from another hierarchy: one of merit, learning, and status."[36] Since the meritocracy is supposed to fairly reward people for their talent and intelligence, it allows people to not think about the role of inherited wealth or preexisting poverty and inequality. Moreover, higher education has become dominated by the quest for elite status, and so the educational system itself becomes part of the structure that produces winners and losers. The combination then of meritocracy and capitalistic competition helps to produce a winner-takes-all economy that seems fair to liberals on the surface.

Frank also highlights meritocratic narcissism when he comments on how the writer David Brooks complemented President Obama for surrounding himself with an educational elite: "It was the educational pedigree of the then-forming Team Obama that won the columnist's esteem. Nearly every person Brooks mentioned—the new president's economic advisers, his foreign policy advisers, even the first lady—had collected a degree from an Ivy League institution, more than one in most cases. The new administration would be a 'valedictocracy', Brooks joked: 'rule by those who graduate first in their high school classes'."[37] At first glance, it seems wrong to criticize the president for hiring well-educated people, but when we realize the connection between wealth and merit in our society, we see that the obsession with educational status is often a way of excluding large parts of the population from consideration. In appointing high-merit people to work with other highly meritorious people, one creates an echo chamber of shared ideas and values. Moreover, we know that a key to obsessional narcissism is the desire to be seen as complying with the social system, and so the meritocratic structure caters to people who conform without necessarily believing in what they are conforming to.[38] In fact, one reason why liberals attack politicians on the Left is that the liberals do not accept anyone who really believes in what they believe. By calling activists ideologues or extremists, liberal moderates have been able to demonize any truly progressive alternative, and as Hedges insists, the real fault of the liberal class is the rejection of the radical Left and the handing over to the Right all concerns for the working class, poverty, and wages.

For Frank, the liberal abandonment of workers and the rejection of progressive alternatives are hidden by the creation of a meritocratic ideology that pretends not to be an ideology or belief system. Thus, we see in Frank's discussion of the people President Obama decided to hire, how the meritocracy often defines itself as being neutral and fair and therefore outside of ideology and politics: "And on that day in 2008 when Brooks beheld the incoming Obama crew, with their Harvard-certified talent—Lord!—he just about swooned. 'I find myself tremendously impressed by the Obama transition', he wrote. Why? Because 'they are picking the best of the Washington insiders': 'open-minded individuals' who are 'not ideological' and who exhibit lots of 'practical creativity'. They were 'admired professionals', the very best their respective disciplines had to offer. Brooks did not point out that choosing so many people from the same class background—every single one of them, as he said, was a professional—might by itself guarantee closed minds and ideological uniformity. Nobody else pointed this out, either. We always overlook the class interests of professionals because we have trouble thinking of professionals as a 'class' in the first place; like David Brooks, we think of them merely as 'the best'. They are where they are because they are so smart, not because they've been born to an earldom or something."[39] Meritocratic narcissism thus functions here to separate professionalism from class and politics as intelligence and elite education are used as the main markers for success. This promotion of a nonideological ideology in the form of moderate pragmatism can serve to dismiss anyone who challenges the status quo. For instance, one of the main criticisms that Hillary Clinton and her supporters directed at Bernie Sanders was that he was a utopian idealist who did not know how to get things done. In contrast to Sanders, Clinton stressed her experience as part of the elite status quo, and even when she tried to dress herself up in the rhetoric of social justice, her general attitude towards Sanders' progressive policies was to declare that they were impossible, and it was harmful to sell impressionable young people on false hopes.

Clinton's rejection of the progressive alternative should be related to the obsessional narcissistic fear of real change and the focus on conforming to a system of knowledge that is already there. In this structure, individuals are afraid of encountering the unknowable future and the undefined desires of others, and so the unconscious strategy is to place already-known knowledge in front of any new experience. The obsessional, then, complies with the other and works himself or herself to death in order to conform to preestablished paths of knowledge and behavior. This emphasis on intelligence in the neoliberal information economy and the educational meritocracy caters to the obsessional quest for total knowledge. According to Freud, what helps to define the obsessional is a drive for knowing; therefore, the obsessionals have a hard time sleeping at night because they want to figure everything out in their head, and yet there are limits to knowledge, and so they engage in the impossible quest of trying to force the world into preestablished categories.[40]

OBSESSIONAL UNDERSTANDING

For Freud, the original cause for this obsessive quest to understand everything through knowledge is derived from the child's desire to understand sexuality. In the case of the Rat Man, Freud argues that his patient had an "obsession for understanding" that drove everyone around him crazy.[41] Furthermore, Freud traces this obsessional need to understand to an underlying sense of doubt that questions the intentions of others and even one's own intentions.[42] From this perspective, the more our society tries to turn everything into knowledge and information, the more unconscious doubt it generates, which in turn, calls for more knowledge in an obsessive way. It is important to remember that for Lacan, there is a fundamental conflict between Symbolic knowledge and the Real, and what the obsessional tries to do is to anticipate the Real and the desire of others by using knowledge to prepare for an eventual encounter with the unexpected.[43] According to Lacan's theory, the Real is impossible to Symbolize, and so there is a fundamental opposition between the Symbolic order of language and the unknowability of the Real. For instance we can think of education and the World Wide Web as the main current sources for pre-established Symbolic knowledge that can be applied to any situation, and yet, this knowledge is never enough, and the object of desire always remains just out of reach. All knowledge thus produces doubt because the Symbolic is never able to attain the Real, and for the obsessional, Freud insists that the object of desire always remains impossible.

This insatiable drive for knowledge in obsessional narcissism and the educational meritocracy points to how reason can be transformed into rationalizations. Therefore, instead of reason playing a key role in the scientific discovery of new knowledge, Freud points out that the obsessional rationalizes irrational behavior after the fact.[44] Moreover, Freud emphasizes that a central difference between hysterics and obsessionals is that in the case of the former the affect remains manifest and the knowledge is repressed, while in the latter case, the knowledge is manifest but the affect is repressed. In other words, obsessionals may know the traumatic causes of their symptoms, but they have separated off their emotional responses, and so they act as spontaneous Cartesians who promote pure knowledge over emotion.[45]

This splitting off of knowledge from affect can be related to the criticism that liberal politicians like President Obama tend to promote politics in a rational and non-emotional way, and this makes their communication to the public ineffective.[46] Likewise, many liberal professors lecture to students by just giving them the facts, but many students can only be engaged if the communication involves an emotional aspect. As Lacan argued, we live in a period dominated by the discourse of the university where knowledge is placed in a position of agency, and this Symbolic knowledge is directed toward an impossible Real.[47] In other words, we want to Symbolize through idealized knowledge all aspects of ourselves and the world around us, but Symbolic knowledge can never fully represent reality. Here we see how obsessional narcissism dominates our culture and caters to meritocratic narcissism.

In referring to the role of repression in obsessional neurosis, Freud adds that there are two kinds of knowledge for this type of patient: he knows things because he has not forgotten them, but he does not know things because he does not acknowledge their significance.[48] From this perspective, we can say that liberal obsessional narcissists are aware of the problems of poverty and inequality, but they just do not know about these issues on a personal, affective level. This splitting of Symbolic knowledge off from personal experience and conviction can be related to the fact that most politicians in the U.S. Congress are millionaires. Since they do not have struggle on a daily basis with low wages, poor healthcare, and contingent labor, they may have an intellectual understanding of the working class, but they lack a lived, affective connection to people outside of their class.

Returning to the case of the Rat Man, we learn that this patient was haunted by the impulsive idea that if he thought about seeing a woman naked, his father would die.[49] Freud points out that this patient's father was already dead, but what his symptom revealed was that he could only think about enjoyment if it was coupled with guilt. In other terms, obsessional narcissists suffer from guilty pleasure, and the more they try to repress their desires, the stronger their superego becomes. The only defense against this combination of desire and guilt is the production of defensive actions of purification. For example, the obsessional who has to constantly wash his hands is trying to wash away the guilt that is derived from compulsive desire. In the case of liberals, we can see that their efforts to show their moral goodness through acts of conspicuous morality represent an attempt to replace their guilty pleasures with a process of purification, but these efforts always fail.

The liberal personality is then trapped in a vicious cycle where each effort to convince oneself that one is good results in guilt over one's unconscious desires. For instance, the more a company tries to whitewash its destructive effects on the environment or its exploitation of workers, the more its board members feel guilty. Since the good self has to be split off from the bad self, there is no way to recognize the essential ambivalence and complexity of our capitalist existence and meritocratic elitism. From a psychoanalytic perspective, people have to confront their own complicity in the system and bring together the good and bad aspects of their personality, but the obsessional narcissist functions by constantly trying to separate the good self-image from the awareness of guilt, hostility, and immoral desire. Liberal politicians therefore have a difficult time recognizing their role in the destructive aspects of meritocratic capitalism because they cannot tolerate the negative self-image that is generated from their complicity with the system. In this context, educational meritocracy represents an unmitigated good that helps to shield the self from seeing one's role in producing and maintaining inequality.

In response to this obsessional and narcissistic distortion of inner reality and outer truth, Freud argues in the Rat Man case that the only solution is to use free association to help the patient discover the root cause of his impulsive thoughts and defensive actions.[50] For Freud, the ultimate cause of guilty pleasure is the fact that the obsessional experienced as a child the trauma of sexuality with too much enjoyment, and later this strong sexual impulse was countered by the moral need to see the self as good and repress all shameful feelings.[51] However, not only does the Rat Man obsess about his immoral desires, but he also has a difficult time discussing his connection to violence and hostility. For example, when he tries to tell Freud about a horrible scene of torture that his commanding officer was rumored to perform, he breaks off his discourse and has to be reassured by Freud that analysis only works if one gives up one's resistance to speaking about horrible things.[52] When the Rat Man then continues to discuss this scene of torture, Freud remarks that the patient displayed a "horror at pleasure of his own of which he himself was unaware."[53] Here we find the key symptom of the obsessional narcissist: these patients suffer from an unconscious combination of pleasure and hostility. Not only do they repress their own guilty desires, but they unconsciously enjoy their own repressed hostility.

A great example of the emergence of the unconscious enjoyment of hostility can be found in Hillary Clinton's laughter after she announced that the Libyan leader Gaddafi had been murdered. Here Clinton unintentionally exposed the dark underside of American liberalism, which has found great enjoyment in making other people in other countries suffer. Clinton's investment in military engagement should not be seen as a personal flaw; rather, the liberal class has often been invested in a sadistic enjoyment in seeing discounted others suffer. Moreover, at the same time, liberals like Hillary Clinton bemoan the lack of gun control in the U.S., they continue to support supplying the most repressive regimes with weapons. From a Freudian perspective, we can say that the foreign enemy represents a split off bad object that the ego is allowed to attack without losing its own sense of goodness and purity.

In terms of American politics, liberals need conservatives in order to have a clearly identified enemy. For instance, the great joy that liberals get from making fun of Donald Trump and other Republicans reveals the hostility of the good liberal self. Liberals often turn to humor and popular culture in order to express their repressed aggression in a safe social context. Instead of realizing their own role in the destructive aspects of neoliberal society, they are able to identify their political rival as the bad other as they remain internally pure. One of the effects of this structure is that conservatives and liberals need each other since they both define their own group against the other group. Although we are used to seeing a sharp distinction between liberals and conservatives, here we see how they are two sides of the same neoliberal coin.

The splitting off of aggression is discussed by Freud when he shows how the Rat Man's hostility was directed at his superior, Freud, and his dead father.[54] Thus, at the same time, the obsessional narcissist appears to conform to idealized authority figures, there is an underlying hostility that is connected to a fantasy of aggression; however, the need to purify the ego forces this aggression into the unconscious where it comes out in distorted and disowned ways. In the context of meritocratic capitalism and obsessional narcissism, the Other is always a source of competition and hostility, and therefore as Freud tells the Rat Man, each person we admire, we also hate because of their ambition and their ability to take away the objects of our desire.[55]

THE FAILURES OF THE THERAPEUTIC LEFT

The theory of liberal meritocratic narcissism that I am presenting here can be seen as very disillusioning. It appears to support the idea that liberals only act out of guilt and their actions are full of hypocritical contradictions.

Moreover, in following Freud, I have espoused that behind every good intention, there is usually a hostile impulse, and even acts of charity and kindness harbor deep resentment. Yet, psychoanalysis also tells us that we can overcome this unconscious guilt and aggression if we stop trying to maintain a purified self-image and a belief in moral purity. By affirming ambivalence and complexity, we are better able to interact with others without trying to split ourselves and the world into all-good and all-bad parts.

From this psychoanalytic perspective, it is also vital to recognize the problems caused by the current liberal investment in empathy as another way to express one's own goodness to others. Many academic thinkers have recently argued that empathy is the key to positive social change, but psychoanalysis tells us that the belief that we can fully understand the suffering of others often represents a patronizing act that blinds us from realizing that we are simply projecting our own beliefs and understandings onto others.[56] For example, in cases of charity and progressive social programs, what often causes them to fail is that the professional experts feel superior to the people they are trying to help, and this superiority comes from the meritocratic view of expertise and education. We see this conflict between good intentions and bad effects in the case of many aid programs in Africa where the experts fail to really take into account the facts on the grounds and the real needs of the people. For example, many aid programs have pushed developing countries to produce crops for export that the people of the developing country do not eat. Moreover, many military invasions of countries have been pursued in part because the invading country wants to bring democracy or development to a place where it is seen as missing. However, as the U.S. army found in Iraq, the cultural conflicts on the ground may conflict with the expert knowledge of intelligence officers. From this perspective, regime change almost always fails because it is centered on the false understanding of the invading country.

Although many people connect the idea of empathy to psychotherapy and even psychoanalysis, it should be clear that analysis is about people understanding themselves on an affective and cognitive level and not some superior other telling people what they need to know. In fact, in a note to the Rat Man case, Freud argues that progress is only made in analysis when the patient has a personal conviction about unconscious formations, and even if an obsessional patient shows an intellectual understanding of an issue, things will only change if there is also an emotional commitment.[57] Freud points out in this case that is through the transference that one has a chance to combine knowledge with affect and discover the underlying unconscious hostility and desire. This theory of analytic practices is presented when Freud mentions that the Rat Man had met Freud's daughter on the way to one of his sessions: "She had pleased him and he pictured to himself that the only reason why I was kind and incredibly patient with him was that I wanted him as a son-in-law."[58] In this idealizing narcissistic transference, the Rat Man imagines himself to be loveable by placing Freud in the position of the ego ideal, and in this fantasized relationship, the patient repeats and reverses his repressed conflict concerning his father's disapproval of his original love object. Since the Rat Man desires to marry a poor woman, but his father wanted him to marry someone wealthy, the Rat Man was unable to make a choice and "decided" to get sick in order to avoid the issue.[59] In imagining that Freud wanted him to marry his daughter, the Rat Man sought to resolve his problem, but he could only do this by idealizing Freud and imagining that his father would approve of Freud's daughter because she came from a wealthy family. Freud adds that: "At the same time he raised the wealth and position of my family to a level which agreed to the model he had in his mind."[60] Here the transference represents an idealization of the other through a fantasy of the exaggerated wealth of the analyst. From this perspective, the obsessional narcissist is divided between a compulsion to conform to the social ideal and a desire that transgresses the social law.

After Freud examines how the working through the transference was essential to helping this patient deal with his ambivalence concerning his father and his lover, we are told that the Rat Man had a dream where he imagined that Freud's daughter was in front of him with "patches of dung instead of eyes."[61] Freud interprets this transference dream as stating that the Rat Man wants to marry his daughter not because of her wealth. In other words, money has turned to shit, and this serves to reverse the anal economy where the giving of the feces to the parents in toilet training represents the primary act of gift giving. Once again, we see here how underneath acts of altruism and gift giving, we find an underlying hostility.

Freud argues in this case that the ultimate source for the Rat Man's hostility comes from his shame over masturbation.[62] His hostility toward his father is then derived from placing his father in the position of the one who forbids self-satisfaction, and so any type of sexual enjoyment must be equated with a defiance of his father and a repressed wish that this intervening Other would die.[63] Freud adds that the Rat Man had a curious habit of opening up his door late at night "as though his father was standing outside it," and then he would take out his penis and "look at it in the looking-glass."[64] Here we find the ultimate scene of the narcissistic transference: the patient exposes himself in the mirror as he anticipates the look of his ideal dead father. As Lacan emphasizes, the dead father is the ego ideal because this idealized Other can only verify the subject's narcissistic display and is unable to criticize the subject because he is no longer alive.[65]

This display of narcissistic exhibitionism is coupled with the fact that the Rat Man was unable to do work while his father was alive, but once he was dead, he became very productive.[66] Freud states that on the one hand, the Rat Man wanted to please his father by complying with the demand to work, but on another level, he was clearly defying the father's prohibitions.[67] Freud interprets this scene then as the key to the Rat Man's ambivalent relationship with his father and other authority figures, and he traces it back to another scene from the Rat Man's childhood where he was beaten by his father for doing something naughty.[68] In response to this abuse, the Rat Man started to scream in rage and startled his father. The Rat Man relates that after this outburst, he changed and became a coward "out of the fear of the violence of his own rage."[69] This fear of one's own rage can help us to understand the underlying pathology of obsessional narcissists: they are afraid of the criticism and anger of others because they have a horror of their own hostility. In fact, Freud relates that toward the end of the analysis, the Rat Man "began heaping the grossest and filthiest abuse upon me and my family . . . "[70] Here we see how the negative transference allows the patient to work through their underlying aggression in a safe environment.

THE UNCONSCIOUS HOSTILITY OF THE LIBERAL CLASS

Returning to the pathology of liberal obsessional narcissism, we discover that underneath all of the meritocratic ideals, we find a deep-seated hostility for those who exist outside the realm of professional credentialing. According to Frank, the liberal meritocracy is based on constituting an idealized in-group and relegating all others to a debased and neglected status: "Which is to say, a social order supported by test scores and advanced degrees and defended by the many professional associations that have been set up over the years to define correct practice, enforce professional ethics, and wage war on the unlicensed."[71] The liberal meritocracy then not only feeds the self-idealization and self-protection of the winners of the talent and education competition, but it also produces a disavowed hostility toward all of the losers of the professional meritoc-racy. For instance, in higher education, tenured professors are rewarded for conforming to the expected professional standards, but the majority of faculty without the possibility of tenure are devalued and excluded from professional concern or benefits.

This focus on professional standards and licensing has played a major role in psychoanalysis and is at the center of Lacan's critique of American psycho-analysis and American culture. Lacan argues that immigrant analysts escap-ing Europe during World War II were motivated to assimilate to the American way of life and solidify their profession by standardizing psycho-analysis and ultimately submitting it to psychiatry and the medical profes-sion.[72] Lacan posits that this focus on assimilation showed up in the analytic practice where ego psychologists argued that patients should identify with the conflict-free, reality-testing ego of their analysts. Therefore, just as the analyst were identifying with American culture, they were also motivating their patients to identify with them. Psychoanalysis then became a discourse of obsessional narcissistic conformity and normalization, and so the practice itself participated in the repression of unconscious hostility and desire. Moreover, the credentialed analysts attacked the other analysts for not being part of the same professional standards. They also excluded Lacan for not following the standard model of treatment and diagnosis, and eventually kicked him out of the International Psychoanalytic Association.

For Frank, professionals and professional organizations represent the essential social structures of the neoliberal meritocracy: "Professionals are the people who know what ails us and who dispense valuable diagnoses. Professionals predict the weather. They organize our financial deals and determine the rules of engagement. They design our cities and draw the traffic patterns through which the rest of us travel. Professionals know when someone is guilty of a moral or criminal misdeed and they also know precisely what form of retribution that culpability should take."[73] Here we see how knowledge and professional monopolies collude to promote the narcissism of the meritocracy and the exclusiveness of liberal elitism; mean-while, the liberal class plays the role of the superego, which judges the ability of the ideal ego to live up to the cultural standards of the ego ideal.

As the liberal professional class shames anyone who fails to attain the meritocratic ideal, the liberal class itself turns into a structure of confor-mity and exclusion: "Although we are the subjects of all these diagnoses and prescriptions, the group to which professionals ultimately answer is not the public but their peers (and, of course, their clients). They listen mainly to one another. The professions are autonomous; they are not required to heed voices from below their circle of expertise."[74] Liberal professionals then participate in a mirroring system of Imaginary discourse where they only have to listen to each other and not to people they consider to be beneath them or outside of their professional circles.

Frank argues that the professional meritocracy ideally works if the experts remain disinterested and not driven by personal profit or power: "From ship captains to neurosurgeons, modern society depends heavily on people with technical expertise. And so nations grant professionals their elevated status, the sociological theory continues, in exchange for a promise of public service. The professions are supposed to be disinterested occupations or even 'social trustees'; unlike other elements of society, they are not supposed to be motivated by profit or greed. This is why we still find advertising by lawyers and doctors somewhat off-putting, and why Americans were once shocked to learn that radio personalities took money to play records they didn't genuinely like: professionals are supposed to answer to a spirit more noble than personal gain. With the rise of the postindustrial economy in the last few decades, the range of professionals has exploded."[75] Frank represents here the core ideal of modern science and professional ethics, which is that truth is supposed to be pursued regardless of self-interest, and therefore it is necessary to constitute a separation between the professions and capitalism. However, in our current neoliberal meritocracy, science and capitalism are being combined as education, medicine, and law become a source for increased personal profit. As the exchange value replaces all other values in neoliberal culture, the professions lose their objectivity, neutrality, and universality and therefore undermine public trust.

The elite liberal political class also loses its legitimacy by its concentration on supporting professionals rather than working-class people or the poor. Moreover, Frank insists that this focus on careerism has undermined these professions from within: "But what happens when an entire category of experts stops thinking of itself as 'social trustees'? What happens when they abuse their monopoly power? What happens when they start looking mainly after their own interests, which is to say, start acting as a class?"[76] Frank's analysis of the professional class here dovetails with his analysis of the Democrats and the liberal class because all of these social groups have been combined together: "Today, liberalism is the philosophy not of the sons of toil but of the 'knowledge economy' and, specifically, of the knowledge economy's winners: the Silicon Valley chieftains, the big university systems, and the Wall Street titans who gave so much to Barack Obama's

2008 campaign."[77] As Frank points out throughout his book, the big change in the Democratic Party is their abandonment of a focus on policies that would benefit working-class and poor people; however, what Frank does not delve into is the unconscious guilt that is found in the members of the liberal professional class who act as if they are above the common, unlicensed workers. For example, in the following passage, he emphasizes the idealization of the professional class, but he does not mention the underlying unconscious guilt: "Put it a different way: what does it mean when the dominant constituency of the left party in a two-party system is a high-status group rather than the traditional working class? One thing we know for sure that it means is soaring inequality. When the left party in a system severs its bonds to working people—when it dedicates itself to the concerns of a particular slice of high-achieving affluent people—issues of work and income inequality will inevitably fade from its list of concerns."[78] Frank argues that Democrats may still talk about inequality and the working class, but it is clear that their commitment is not with any real type of economic redistribution that would challenge their own wealth and status, yet this explanation is incomplete if we do not add that the abandonment of the working class is coupled with unconscious guilt that is then shouted down by acts of progressive posturing.

The psychoanalytic interpretation I am proposing helps us to understand why Democrats have been able to promote social causes, like gay rights, at the same time they attack progressive economic policies as unrealistic. Here we see that on a global level, identity politics often hides concerns for class and economic injustice. In fact, one can argue that in the 2016 U.S. presidential election, Hillary Clinton focused on issues of race and gender, while Bernie Sanders emphasized inequality and the power of the "Billionaire Class." Or to be more precise, Clinton was able to gain voters because they saw her as the natural ally of women and people of color even though most of her past policies and positions have not helped these groups.

Clinton's great strategic move was to tie herself closely to President Obama so that she could not only bring in the African-American vote, but any criticism Sanders made of her would be seen as a criticism of the first black president. This strategy was purely psychological because it relied on creating the identification between Clinton and Obama: just as Bill Clinton was labeled by Toni Morrison to be the first black president, Hillary made herself black through association.[79] It did not matter that she had promoted policies in the past that undermined African Americans, what mattered was that on the level of psychological identity, she was considered to be black.

As a Sanders supporter, I had many opportunities to engage in conversations with the liberal supporters of Hillary Clinton, and what I found so interesting was that they virtually never discussed what policies Clinton had supported in the past or her actions as Secretary of State; instead, they said she had experience, Sanders was a utopian idealist, and the most important thing to do was defeat Donald Trump. The focus of this liberal conformity was then on an emotional and symbolic level: people feared Trump, and they supported the status quo, but on a fundamental level, they did not think that any real change could ever happen.

From a psychoanalytic perspective, it is important to point out that since obsessional narcissists tend to repress their emotional responses by focusing on their own intellectual knowledge, the liberal supporters of Clinton projected their own emotional politics onto the supporters of Sanders. In other words, the liberals refused to realize that they were supporting Clinton for largely emotional reasons, but they saw the support for Sanders' rational positions as purely the result of an emotional investment.

Since liberals do not believe that there is any alternative to our current capitalist system, they are able to dismiss a truly Leftist alternative as being purely idealistic and impracticable, and for Frank, it is the meritocracy that helps Democrats justify their abandonment of workers and the poor: "Another term for this understanding of equality is meritocracy, which is one of the great, defining faiths of the professional class. Meritocracy is about winners, and ensuring that everyone has a chance to become one. 'The areas in which the left has made the most significant progress', writes the journalist Chris Hayes, '—gay rights, inclusion of women in higher education, the end of de jure racial discrimination—are the battles it has fought or is fighting in favor of making the meritocracy more meritocratic. The areas in which it has suffered its worst defeats—collective action to provide universal public goods, mitigating rising income inequality—are those that fall outside the meritocracy's purview'."[80] Since the meritocratic system focuses on rewarding the achievements of individuals, it has a hard time recognizing the need for collective action to reverse systemic inequalities. Moreover, as Frank points out, the people making policy decisions are all meritocratic winners, and so they see no need in changing the system: "Another reason we know that a party of professionals will care little about inequality is because professionals themselves care little about it. While this segment of the population tends to be very liberal on questions of civil liberties and sexual mores, the sociologist Steven Brint tells us that professionals are 'not at all liberal on economic and equality-related issues'. On anything having to do with organized labor, as we shall see, they are downright conservative."[81] It is thus no accident that Democrats have failed to spend their political capital on protecting the rights of workers to unionize and negotiate for better wages and benefits. After all, in a meritocracy, wages are set by the judgment of individual talent and not some prearranged collective agreement.

One of the great mysteries that Frank does not fully explore is why the very groups that have been abandoned by the Democratic Party continue to vote for liberal politicians. For instance, why did so many unions come out early to support Clinton, and why did so many women and African Americans voice their faithful support for her? Part of the explanation for people voting against their own self-interest must be due to a lack of knowledge about actual policies and their effects. However, even when union leaders acknowledged that the Democrats have not made unionization and workers' rights a priority for 50 years, they still voiced their strong support for Hillary. Of course, as we saw above, part of this response is related to the fear of the conservative alternative, but what explains unions not getting behind Bernie Sanders?

As a union president who supported Sanders, I had the opportunity to debate many union supporters of Clinton, and what I found was that they were driven by three emotional responses: (1) the Republicans are evil and only Hillary can beat them; (2) Sanders policies are utopian and impossible, and he can never win; and (3) deep down, Hillary is a progressive. I call these responses emotional because they are not based on actual facts and policies; instead they are centered on fear, resignation, and hope. Yet, when Sanders supporters tried to point out the irrational and emotional foundation of many Hillary supporters, they were called sexists, and so once again, we are faced with the ability of identity politics to trump class politics. Liberals then need identity groups to not only solidify their base but also to reject any type of criticism: if one criticizes the past policies and actions of Hillary Clinton, one is a sexist and a racist, and if one criticizes any of her followers, one is also a racist and a sexist.

My argument is not to deny that our society is still shaped by racism and sexism; rather, the point is to see how these destructive psychological forces can be used politically. In the case of conservatives, they often deny racism and sexism in order to argue against the welfare state, while liberals not only use race and sex to attract supporters but also to defend against critics.

In this political culture, Sanders was placed in an impossible position because if he tried to distinguish his policies from Clinton's, he was seen as being a sexist and racist who was helping to elect an evil Republican. Moreover, throughout her campaign against Sanders, Clinton appropriated many of his major ideas in order to show that both candidates were really saying the same thing except she had a more realistic approach and the experience to get things done. In fact, many of her liberal supporters bought into her campaign rhetoric because they adopted a cynical ideology, which is based on the idea that in our current system, no real change can ever really happen, and so it is best to rely on someone who at least we know has the experience and knowledge to maintain the status quo. However, for many of Sanders' supporters, Clinton cannot be trusted because she is only saying things to get elected and her past record does not match her current rhetoric.

For Frank it is the self-idealization of liberals that blinds them from seeing the harm caused by their investment in meritocratic justice: "Nor can the leaders of the professional class see the absurdity of urging everyone else to do exactly as they themselves did to make their way to the top. It is as if some oil baron were to proclaim that the unemployed could solve their problems if they just found good places to drill for oil. Or if some mutual-fund manager were to suggest that the solution to inequality was for everyone to put their savings in the stock market."[82] Since the obsessional narcissist has to be idealized by an ideal cultural Other to have his or her ideal ego reinforced, it is necessary to conform to the social system as one convinces oneself that one is an isolated individual rewarded for individual talent and skills. A society then led by professional elites will be a society centered on conformity and the idealizing and mirroring transference to idealized Others.

The only way to counter the type of conformity to an idealizing political ideology I have articulated in this chapter is to expose the underlying unconscious fears and desires that support the neoliberal status quo. To further understand this political structure, I will in the next chapter show how the presidential campaign of Donald Trump represents the unveiling of the repressed aspects of the conservative coalition. Like a good psychoanalysis, Trump's free associations reveal the truth by exposing the fantasies supporting symptomatic identifications. Although Trump appears to be a continuation of the conservative coalition, we shall see that he actually represents the end of this political formation because he lacks the shame that usually prevents one from saying the truth, and the truth that he exposes is that the repressed driving force behind American politics is the headless, heedless capitalist drive.

NOTES

1. Lacan, J. (1998). *The four fundamental concepts of psycho-analysis* (Vol. 11). New York: WW Norton & Company, p. 257.
2. Piketty, T. (2014). *Capital in the twenty-first century.* Cambridge, MA: Harvard University Press.
3. Zwick, R. (2004). Is the SAT a 'wealth test?' The link between educational achievement and socioeconomic status. In *Rethinking the SAT: The future of standardized testing in university admissions* (pp. 203–216).
4. Marsh, J. (2011). *Class dismissed: Why we cannot teach or learn our way out of inequality.* New York: NYU Press.
5. Easterly, W. (2013). *The tyranny of experts: Economists, dictators, and the forgotten rights of the poor.* New York: Basic Books.
6. Kernberg, O.F. (1985). *Borderline conditions and pathological narcissism.* New York: Rowman & Littlefield.
7. Freud, S. (1963). *Three case histories.* New York: Collier Books.
8. Ibid, p. 20.
9. Beck, J.S. (1979). *Cognitive therapy.* New York: John Wiley & Sons, Inc.
10. Freud, S. (1963). Dynamics of the transference. In *Therapy and technique* (p. 107). New York: Collier Books.
11. Freud, *Three case*, p. 20.
12. Lacan, J. (1998). *The four fundamental concepts of psycho-analysis* (Vol. 11). New York: WW Norton & Company, pp. 224–225.
13. Freud, *Three case, p. 20.*
14. Ibid.
15. Lacan, *The four*, p. 257.
16. Kohut, H. (2013). *The analysis of the self: A systematic approach to the psychoanalytic treatment of narcissistic personality disorders.* Chicago: University of Chicago Press.
17. Lacan, *The four fundamental*, pp. 230–243.
18. Freud, S. (1949). *An outline of analysis.* New York: Norton, p. 32.
19. Freud, S., (1963). On narcissism: An introduction. In *General psychological theory.* New York: Collier Books.
20. Kohut, H. (2009). *How does analysis cure?* Chicago: University of Chicago Press, p. 64.
21. Lacan, *The four fundamental*, pp. 244–260.
22. Motley, M.T. (1995). *Overcoming your fear of public speaking.* New York: McGraw-Hill College.
23. Freud, S. (1961). *The ego and the id.* New York: Norton, p. 33.

24. Freud, *Three case*, p. 37.
25. Ibid.
26. Ibid., p. 17.
27. Easterly, W. (2013). *The tyranny of experts: Economists, dictators, and the forgotten rights of the poor.* New York: Basic Books.
28. Lacan, J., & Sheridan, A. (2001). *Écrits: A selection.* New York: Norton, p. 13.
29. Hedges, C. (2011). *Death of the liberal class.* Vintage Books Canada.
30. Marsh, J. (2011). *Class dismissed: Why we cannot teach or learn our way out of inequality.* New York: NYU Press.
31. Frank, *Listen*, p. 19.
32. Lander, C. (2008). *Stuff white people like: A definitive guide to the unique taste of millions.* New York: Random House.
33. Brooks, D. (2010). *Bobos in paradise: The new upper class and how they got there.* New York: Simon and Schuster.
34. Frank, *Listen*, p. 15.
35. Frank, *Listen*, p. 15.
36. Ibid., p. 16.
37. Ibid., p. 20.
38. Frank, R.H. (2016). *Success and luck: Good fortune and the myth of meritocracy.* Princeton: Princeton University Press.
39. Frank, *Listen*, p. 21.
40. Lacan argues that we now live in a period, which is dominated by the agency of symbolic knowledge and what he calls the discourse of the university. Lacan, J., Miller, J.A., & Grigg, R. (2007). *The seminar of Jacques Lacan. Book 17, The other side of psychoanalysis.* New York: Norton.
41. Freud, *Three case*, p. 48.
42. Ibid., p. 50.
43. Lacan, J. (1949). The mirror stage as formative of the function of the I as revealed in psychoanalytic experience. In *Ecrits: A selection* (pp. 1–7).
44. Freud, *Three case*, p. 58.
45. Ibid., p. 54.
46. Westen, D. (2008). *Political brain: The role of emotion in deciding the fate of the nation.* New York: Public Affairs.
47. Lacan, *The other side*.
48. Freud, *Three case*, p. 54, note 33.
49. Ibid., p. 23.
50. Ibid., p. 25.
51. Ibid., p 26.
52. Ibid., p. 26.
53. Ibid., p. 27.
54. Ibid., pp. 27–28.
55. Ibid., p. 39.

56. For a stress on empathy as the solution to social problems see, Nussbaum, M.C. (2012). *Not for profit: Why democracy needs the humanities*. Princeton: Princeton University Press.
57. Freud, *Three case*, p. 40, note 18.
58. Ibid., p. 57.
59. Ibid., pp. 56–57.
60. Ibid., p. 57.
61. Ibid., p. 58.
62. Ibid., p. 61.
63. Ibid.
64. Ibid.
65. Lacan, J. (1960). The subversion of the subject and the dialectic of desire in the Freudian unconscious. In *Ecrits: A selec*tion (pp. 292–325).
66. Freud, *Three case*, p. 62.
67. Ibid.
68. Ibid.
69. Ibid., p. 63.
70. Ibid., p. 65.
71. Frank, *Listen*, p. 22.
72. Lacan, *Ecrits*, p. 27, p. 37, pp. 306–307.
73. Frank, *Listen*, p. 22.
74. Ibid., p. 23.
75. Ibid.
76. Ibid., p. 25.
77. Ibid., p. 29.
78. Ibid., p. 30.
79. Morrison, T. (1998, October 5). Clinton as the first black president. *The New Yorker*, p. 5.
80. Ibid.
81. Ibid.
82. Ibid., p. 36.

CHAPTER 4

Trump and Sanders on the Couch: Neoliberal Populism on the Left and the Right

Abstract This chapter argues that if we want to fully understand the political popularity of people like Donald Trump, we should return to Freud's theory of the group formation and his notion of emotional identification. As a form of group hypnosis, Right-wing populism relies on followers suspending their critical faculties as they access parts of their unconscious id, and psychoanalysis helps us to understand how these unconscious processes function in political movements.

Keywords Donald Trump · Hypnosis · Bernie Sanders · Populism · Fascism · Reality TV · Surplus value · Primal horde · Freud · Lacan

On one level, we can understand Donald Trump's successful effort to become the Republican presidential nominee as a result of the failure of liberals to align with the working class. In his constant criticism of trade policies and unfair practices by China, Trump tells displaced workers that he will "Make America Great Again" by bringing back jobs and making great deals. Of course, his discourse appears to be pure rhetoric with few actual policy prescriptions, but what has amazed so many pundits, party insiders, and political scientists is that it does not seem to matter to his supporters if his promises cannot be kept; in fact, it is unclear whether they care if his rhetoric has any connection to actual reality. To understand this political discourse,

© The Author(s) 2016
R. Samuels, *Psychoanalyzing the Left and Right After Donald Trump,*
Critical Theory and Practice in Psychology and the Human Sciences,
DOI 10.1007/978-3-319-44808-4_4

I argue that we should return to Freud's theory of the group formation and his notion of emotional identification. In other words, we need a rational theory of the irrational in order to understand how populists on the Right, like Trump, gain and maintain supporters. Moreover, Freud's theory of free association helps us to see how Trump's campaign might actually be good for America because it serves to expose the underlying fantasies that support the conservative coalition. Finally, it is important to place Trump's brand of fascism in the context of contemporary media and neoliberal capitalism as we also examine Bernie Sanders' populism of the Left.

SUSPENDING THE CRITICAL

In *Group Psychology and the Analysis of the Ego*, Freud uses his experience of hypnotizing people to argue that at the foundation of blind love and group psychology, we find the same overestimation of the object and suspension of the subject's critical faculties.[1] Freud claims that in these social situations, one replaces one's moral conscience and critical faculties with the object of identification (the ego ideal). He also posits that this relationship returns the hypnotized follower to a time when the helpless child is dominated by the archaic father and the all-powerful id before the development of the reality-testing ego.

The first way, then, that psychoanalysis helps us to understand the neoliberal populism of the Right and Trump's relation to his followers is through this notion that the identification with the leader functions to suspend the reality-testing function of the followers. As Trump said on several occasions, he could shoot someone in the middle of a crowded street, and his followers would still support him. This mode of blind love and adoration perplexes his critics who cannot understand how he is not held accountable for saying outrageous things. From the perspective of the rational, reality-testing ego, it is absurd to suggest that he could get away with murder, but on the level of political identification, reality can be constructed purely through speech acts that go beyond reason and perception.

For Lacan, the structure of hypnosis represents the key to understanding fascism and the politics of self-sacrifice. At the end of his *Four Fundamental Concepts of Psychoanalysis*, he opposes psychoanalysis to fascism by arguing that analysis works by maintaining a distance between the idealizing "I" of transference and the object that causes one to desire, while in hypnosis, blind love, and collective fascination, the object and the ideal are superimposed.[2] For instance, in hypnosis, the gaze of the hypnotizer is the object that also plays the role of the ego ideal in the form of suggestion.[3] Lacan posits that Freud developed this theory of hypnotic fascination at the time of his growing awareness of fascism, and so Freud in his text on group psychology uses hypnosis to explain the rise of social formations that will eventually result in Nazism.[4] Moreover, since psychoanalytic practice grew out of the abandonment of hypnosis, Lacan is able to argue that the discourse of the analyst offers a critique of hypnosis and fascism.[5] Thus, while the structure of fascination is based on the identification of the ego ideal with the object, analysis is centered on the separation of the two. In the practice of psychoanalysis, by not responding to the demands of the patient's desire for identification and idealization, the transference based on fascination is suspended. In other words, the analyst has to desire not to be idealized by the subject, and in this way, Lacan adds, it is the analyst who occupies the position of the hypnotized in an upside-down hypnosis.[6]

With regard to Trump, once his followers place him in the position of the Ideal ego, and they identify with this ideal, they give up their critical faculties as they become fascinated with the power of his voice. Like the lover who has overestimated the love-object, one becomes humble and blind as one follows the commands of the beloved.[7] For Freud, in terms of the formation of a fascist group, what occurs is that the followers all identify on an emotional level with being in the same situation.[8] In this case, the people being imitated, the other followers, no longer represent a love interest, but rather, the group unifies by sharing the same emotional response through a process Freud calls "mental infection."[9] The example Freud gives for this contagious identification concerns a group of girls in a boarding school who all have the same emotional response of jealousy when another girl receives a letter from someone with whom she is secretly in love.[10] Unlike the identification through incorporation or the symptomatic identification with a single trait from another, this third form of identification involves copying an emotional reaction in response to identifying with the desire of others. Since the other girls want to be in the same place as the girl who has received the letter, they all respond in the same emotional way, and under a sense of guilt, they all accept the need to suffer. We find here the essence of the victim identification on a group level: people unite over a shared suffering, which is able to spread in a viral way as a mental infection. It is clear that Trump feeds this type of victim identification by stressing how the working class has been screwed over by bad trade deals, immigrants, and an ineffective government. To understand the populism of the Right, it is therefore necessary to understand both the shared viral emotional identification between the followers and the hypnotic relation between each member and the leader. As Lacan adds, what has plagued the Marxist-Hegelian interpretation of fascism is that it cannot explain these unconscious processes of identification and idealization.[11]

Psychoanalysis helps us to comprehend both Trump and his followers by showing how fascism is structured in the same way as hypnosis, and hypnosis itself replicates blind love.[12] Freud affirms that in all of these social ties, we always witness "the weakness of intellectual ability, the lack of emotional restraint, the incapacity for moderation and delay, the inclination to exceed every limit in the expression of emotion . . . "[13] Here, we find a great description of a Trump rally where the uneducated gather to express their emotions in front of a leader who cannot stop using excessive language. As Freud insists, in this state of group regression, the lack of courage and originality of the members is compensated by the repetition of group attitudes based on "racial characteristics, class prejudices, public opinions."[14] The populism of the Right thus needs prejudice in order to solidify group solidarity and to overcome the followers' lack of courage and originality.

On a fundamental level, Freud argues that at the root of all social solidarity, we find the replacement of envy and jealousy with an identification based on equality.[15] For instance, when a new child is born, and the older child feels that he will lose the love of his parents, his first desire is to eliminate his rival, but he soon realizes that since his parents love the children the same, his only solution is to identify himself with the other child.[16] Here, group identity is formed as a reaction to envy and hostility, and as Freud posits, the desire for social justice and equality stem from the idea of the child that if he cannot be the sole favorite of the parents, then no one should be favored.[17] Freud adds that we find the same dynamic at play when a bunch of girls all crowd around an adored singer: while it would be easy for them to all be jealous of each other; instead they act as a united group and share their sentimental emotions: "Originally rivals, they have succeeded in identifying themselves with one another by means of a similar love for the same object."[18] By moving from Imaginary rivalry to Symbolic identification, the possibility of social solidarity is established. In other words, the dual relationship between the ego and the other is transcended by the Symbolic relationship of language and social mediation.[19]

Freud's theory of social justice can be traced to the same dynamics of overcoming Imaginary envy, rivalry, and jealousy. According to the "group spirit," no one in the social order should put himself forward, and all "must be the same and have the same."[20] Furthermore, in Freud's rewriting of the theory of the social contract, "Social justice means that we deny ourselves many things so that others may to do without them as well . . . The demand for equality is the root of social conscience and the sense of duty."[21] Unlike other thinkers, Freud bases the motives for social justice, solidarity, and the demand for equality on a reaction to envy, jealousy, and rivalry.[22] However, Freud's theory of the social bond may entail that all forms of populism cannot help but rely on irrational group processes.

POPULISM ON THE RIGHT AND THE LEFT

It is important to return to Freud's text to see how the populism of the Right can be related to the populism on the Left. In other terms, how do we explain Trump's appeal to the working class and how does it differ from someone like Bernie Sanders on the Left? I will argue that part of the answer to this question entails distinguishing between the class antagonisms of the Left and the racial divisions of the Right. In the case of the Left, the group solidarity of the people is defined in opposition to the upper classes who control the economy and the political system. On the other hand, the populists on the Right need to define themselves against liberals, immigrants, foreign nations, and different races and ethnicities; instead of focusing on class conflict or class solidarity, they interpret class through the lens of identity politics. In this structure, someone like Trump can argue that if only we built a wall and kept all of the Mexicans out, we would have good jobs. The problem then is not that the billionaire class is hording all of the wealth and profits; the problem is that Mexicans and Chinese are stealing our jobs. In this conservative version of identity politics, white males blame people who do not share the same demographic identity for all of their problems, and we see this dynamic throughout the world where immigrants and Muslims are blamed for the failures of economic globalization.

Unlike populists on the Right who are locked into an Imaginary rivalry with their debased other, Freud's theory implies that populists on the Left overcome interpersonal rivalry by affirming a Symbolic notion of universal justice, but it is unclear if the Left can escape from the idealization of the charismatic leader and the division of society between the idealized people and the demonized powerful others. In other terms, it may be that both the populisms of the Left and the Right rely on a regressive hypnotic structure where blind love negates critical thinking and universal justice.

Freud posits that in social groups like the military and the church, all the members have to be loved by the leader in the same way, but this demand for equality is only for the members and not the leader: "All the members must be equal to one other, but they all want to be ruled by one person."[23] It is, then, this need for an all-powerful leader/master that has to be explained in order to determine how populism functions today. For Freud, the roots of fascism can be understood through his theory of the primal horde that he borrowed from Darwin and first presented in *Totem and Taboo*. In his retelling of his original theory, Freud claims that in this primal social structure, we find the origins of the powerful leaders in relation to a community of equal brothers.[24] He then hypothesizes that what happens in blind love, fascism, and hypnosis is a regression to the state of the primal horde and that there is a homology between the development of the group and the development of the individual.[25] Freud stresses that this primal leader and father was totally free and "his intellectual acts were strong and independent even in isolation and his will needed no reinforcement from others . . . he loved no one but himself, but other people only as far as they served his needs."[26] This analysis by Freud can be read as a perfect description of Trump, who is seen as a powerful leader by his followers because he is strong willed, and he appears to need no one else, not even the Republican Party.

In this reactivation of the primal horde, Trump's wealth allowed him to run without relying on other people or groups, and by self-funding his campaign, he was able to feed the image of the self-made man who is the master of his own destiny. Furthermore, his wealth gives him the power to treat other people as objects of his will: his team is only there to service his needs as he presents himself as the isolated leader, uninfluenced by the usual political donors or party leaders. In referring to Nietzsche, and with the rising power of fascism in mind, Freud calls this type of leader a "superman," who is someone who loves no one but is loved by all: "He may be of a masterful nature, absolutely narcissistic, self-confident, and independent."[27] Once again, this description fits Trump well and shows how the populism of the Right is always dependent on the overestimation of the leader who is a purely independent and self-satisfying master.

Freud argues that love often functions to put a check on narcissism, but with the fascist crowd, there is no limit to the narcissism of the leader.[28] Central to Freud's theory is the idea that the narcissism of the master is coupled with the inhibition of sexual impulses in the followers. Since object love threatens to undermine narcissism, Freud has to find a way to explain both the narcissism of the leader and the sexless devotion of the followers. Moreover, he posits that in order to show how group psychology turns into individual psychology, it is necessary to posit that the primal father has horded all of the women and has prevented his sons from accessing direct sexual pleasure: the result is that the sons have to be abstinent as they watch the father enjoy.[29] Meanwhile, Freud adds that the unused sexual drives of the brothers are transformed into the emotional ties with the father/leader. What is so interesting in this description is that it matches the way that Trump always surrounds himself with beautiful women and family members during his press conferences. He literally represents himself as the primal father of enjoyment as his followers are motivated to identify with the primal enjoyment of the father.[30]

In returning to the question of hypnosis, Freud argues that the hypnotist tells the subject that the hypnotizer possesses a mysterious power that robs people of their free will.[31] Freud posits that this power must be the same that is used by kings and chieftains and makes them difficult to approach. Freud then adds that it is the look of the Other that is the source of power.[32] The look or gaze allows the hypnotist to say to the subject that all attention should be focused on the hypnotist as the rest of the world becomes uninteresting, but the hypnotists does not say this because the relationship has to remain unconscious.[33] For Freud, this situation of focused attention on the Other and disinterest in the rest of the world defines the essence of transference and the functioning of unconscious formations like jokes and dreams.[34] In other words, the sleeper who loses the critical capacity to test reality regresses to a fascist state of hypnosis where the helpless subject is forced to watch the representations that appear to come from the Other.

Freud argues that the hypnotist puts the patient into a state that is similar to dreams because the critical faculties are suspended and the unconscious emerges in a distorted form.[35] This regression also entails that the subject returns to the primal relation between the all-powerful archaic father and the helpless child: "[W]hat is thus awakened is the idea of a paramount and dangerous personality towards who only a passive-masochistic attitude is possible, to whom one's will has to be surrendered –while to be alone with him, 'to look him in the face', appears a hazardous enterprise."[36] Freud insists that the regression to the relationship with the gaze of the threatening, dangerous Other is desired by the subject who wishes to be governed by "unrestricted force."[37] Freud thus posits a primary form of masochism that defines fascism, hypnosis, blind love, and the unconscious itself.

It has been my argument that one cannot explain the political power of someone like Trump, if one does not work through these unconscious processes that determine the fundamental relationship between people and authority. While pundits and political scientists are perplexed by the seductive power of populist leaders, Freud helps us to see how we all contain in our unconscious a masochistic desire to be ruled by a powerful, archaic force. As we saw in Chap. 2, at the roots of many political and religious institutions, we find a fantasy of traumatic victimization, which is then used to give the subject a sense of innocence and purity that allows one to escape from criticism and justifies all acts of revenge. In the fascist crowd, the submission to the leader reactivates the fundamental fantasy of masochistic victimization where pain is confused with pleasure and fiction mixes with reality. However, as Freud and Lacan insist, we are often blind to the force of the unconscious because we are so invested in censoring anything that we perceive to be irrational, shameful, antisocial, or out of our personal control.

HISTORY AND THE UNCONSCIOUS

Up to this point, I have focused on an ahistorical approach to Trump and the political unconscious, but it is important to place the universal structures Freud developed within a historical structure. As many critics have argued, psychoanalysis often suffers from not taking into full account the effect of different cultures and time periods, and so it is necessary to historicize and relativize psychic structures.[38] In the case of analyzing the rise of Trump, it is vital to look at how contemporary capitalism and media culture produces a new mode of fascism.

On the most fundamental level, we can define our current neoliberal order as one that places the exchange value of the market above all other values, meanings, or traditions. As Marx argued, capitalism spreads beyond all borders and liquefies all traditional stable structures, and what we are witnessing in our current age of globalization is the viral movement of capital into all parts of the world and all aspects of human existence. It is therefore important to ask how we must revise Freud's modern theories when they are used to understand a neoliberal world? Specifically for our current purposes, we have to ask: How does modern fascism and the populism of the Right get restructured in the age of global capital and neoliberal mass media?[39]

THE COMMODIFICATION OF THE SELF

As a former reality TV persona, Trump has been able to cash in on his mass media star power, which circles around the commodification of his own identity. What Trump is always selling is his own name and reputation; in fact, he broke new ground when during a press conference after a primary election victory, he brought out several of his own products, including Trump Steaks and Trump Vodka. Here the border between politics and business has been broken down as both are repackaged as advertising brand recognition. In turning his name into his central commodity, Trump himself is able to embody pure surplus value: like so many multinational corporations, instead of focusing on producing products for use-value, Trump sells a brand.[40] However, as a shameless self-promoter, Trump's refusal to differentiate between politics, entertainment, and business threatens to expose the repressed truth of our political system, which concerns the way democracy has been taken over by the need of candidates to spend huge sums of money on advertising themselves like a product. In this historical instance, the modern divide between democracy, capitalism, and entertainment has broken down.

To understand this new form of fascism that we find in neoliberal society, we can turn to Freud's theory of jokes.[41] Freud's basic insight is that the joke teller bribes the audience by giving them enjoyment in exchange for the listeners not criticizing the joke teller or holding the joker responsible for his sexual and aggressive attacks. Here the escape from criticism is not due solely to the submission of the subject to unconscious processes controlled by a powerful censoring source; instead, one makes an implicit social contract that allows for the free reign of unconscious fantasies that cannot be subjected to criticism. In the case of Trump, he sanctions the racism, sexism, and violence of his crowd as they promise not to hold him responsible, but in the process, he himself becomes a joker.

Unlike the fascist leader of the past, someone like Trump undermines his own power by turning himself into a pure surplus value. Instead of following the tradition of other fascist leaders and arguing that America must affirm its destiny and dominate the world through the creation of a master race, he tries to sell himself as a self-made brand dedicated to his own self-inflation. For example, one of the more remarkable aspects of his discourse is his constant use of superlatives, which can be considered to be a form of hyperbolic self-inflated language. As he insists that he is going to make America great again and make the best deals because he has the greatest company with the greatest employees, this hyperbole indicates an excess and lack inherent in language itself.

SANDERS AND THE POPULISM OF THE LEFT

Trump's discourse has to be placed within a historical context that combines together the abandonment of the working class by the Democratic Party and the conservative coalition's use of victim identification politics. Since both sides fear and reject a real Left alternative that would help the working class, the vast majority of the populace is forced to support either Trump or Bernie Sanders. Although Sanders does appear to offer a populism of the Left without the Right's reliance on prejudice and a strong leader, what Sanders actually represents is a fake version of revolution and socialism. Of course, Sanders would try to do more for the working class as he challenges a corrupt campaign finance system and demonizes Wall Street and the wealthy, but many of his policy proposals do not go far enough to take on the destructive effects of neoliberal capitalism. For example, he wants to raise taxes on the rich and financial institutions, but he has no way of stopping the flow of money to other parts of the world. Likewise, he wants to protect American jobs, yet in the current system, individual nations cannot prevent multinational corporations from moving their labor or operations to another country. As I will argue in the next chapter, all of our major social and political issues are now global, but we lack any global government or real enforcement mechanism, and so, the current focus on nation-state solutions will always fail.

In terms of his call for revolution, what Sanders is really doing is encouraging millions of people to donate money online, and while this helps people to buy into the system, it is far from a political revolution. In fact, we are still seeing money-controlled politics, as Sanders has to raise huge funds to air commercials, hire staff, and hold rallies. Moreover, there is polling evidence that many of his supporters are not focused on his actual policy initiatives; rather, they are excited by an alternative, and they fear the other choices.[42] Also, as much as Sanders wants to tell his followers that his campaign is really about the people, they cannot help but invest in a cult of personality. Instead of doing the hard, long work of actually building a viable alternative political organization and movement, the Sanders campaign is often fueled by emotion and temporary involvement.

Sanders' use of the term socialism is also highly problematic because he is not talking about the public owning companies and banks; what he is offering is to rebuild the old welfare state system by publically financing universities and healthcare and breaking up the largest financial institutions. Although this would be a major improvement for the United States, it does not confront the destructive nature of global capitalism or the limitations of global regulation. Also, like so many other liberal politicians, Sanders believes that higher education is the path to a good job, even though it is clear that most jobs are now low-paying service positions that do not require a college degree.

Sanders has been a good counter to Trump's use of racism and xenophobia, but his populism of the Left still relies more on emotion than reason. For instance, his huge rallies are subject to the same contagion of emotion that we find in Trump's crowds, and many of his policy proposals are not matched with any description of how these goals will be achieved; instead he relies on saying that if millions of people get involved, then politicians from both parties will be forced to do the right thing. Unfortunately, a real democratic movement for justice cannot be achieved without a real organization and dedication to radical transformation.

It is also hard to imagine how the current campaign system in America will be changed in the way Sanders and his supporters demand because the Supreme Court has ruled that money is the same thing as speech, and since you cannot regulate free speech, you cannot legislate the use of money in campaigns. What is remarkable about this legal opinion is the way that speech and capitalism are equated. As a prime example of neoliberal culture, what we find in the court's ruling is the idea that speech, freedom, and money are the same thing, and so any form of censorship or governmental control is experienced as a form of Symbolic castration.

THE MYTH OF THE LIBERAL SUPEREGO

Returning to Trump, we see that the false equation of money with speech and freedom is enhanced by the notion that the internal censor in the form of the superego is in actuality the liberal media, professors, and political establishment. Due to a false association between liberals and the social super-ego, what many of his followers like about Trump is that he appears to say what is on his mind without censorship. As he himself indicates, he is tired of all of the political correctness in American society, so he is not going to shy away from calling people terrorists or rapists. Supporters see this type of discourse as indicating that he says the truth without censorship, and he will no longer be a victim of the liberal super-ego that makes us feel guilty for all of our negative thoughts about Mexicans, Muslims, foreigners, and women. From this perspective, the liberal elites who control our media, universities, and political discourse prevent us from saying the truth, and so we are unable to confront our real problems.[43]

This identification of liberal elites with the super-ego is coupled with the idea that in our media-saturated world, we desire a media that is immediate, natural, and real. Thus, reality TV, and many modes of social media, represent attempts of overcoming Symbolic alienation by making the Symbolic mediation itself appear to be natural and immediate. By getting rid of scripts and actors, new media productions pretend that they are presenting the real without mediation. Therefore, as a former reality TV star, Trump tries to cash in on this idea that he is real, authentic, and true because he does not talk from a script, and he refuses to be handled by PR people. In this mode of discourse, he is trying to make the media immediate and overcome alienation and the censorship of the liberal super-ego. It appears that even though he has no political experience and very little knowledge of politics, what people like about him is that he is an anti-politician politician feeding into the anti-government rhetoric of the conservative coalition. After all, since the time of Reagan, one of the main tenants of the Republican Party has been to get rid of government, and so it should not surprise us if Trump can win with no experience. Since conservatives have been demonizing the government for two generations in order to reduce regulations and cut taxes, they are now being subjected to their own medicine. Trump is thus the logical extension of the conservative movement, which was always really about gaining political power and enhancing personal wealth.

Trump then is performing a form of wild analysis where he free associates without much shame or censorship. Since he does not feel that he has to rely on wealthy donors to back his campaign, he is able to say the truth about his party, and this often means exposing its hatred for others. Thus, instead of using indirect racism and sexism, he openly says what he thinks about Mexicans, Muslims, and women. As a verbal bully, he uses words as his main weapon, and these words often end up attacking everyone and anyone, including his own party. For example, in one speech, he commented on how much he loves the uneducated. What he was probably trying to say was that many of his supporters do not have a college education and that is why they are suffering so badly in the current economy, but what he actually revealed was that Republicans often appeal to people who do not believe in reason, expertise, or science.

In this strange political culture, the liberals have abandoned the working class for meritocratic professionals, while the wealthy donors of the Right cash in on their false support for the working class. Not only does a sense of shared victimhood unite the wealthy and the poor on the Right, but as we see with Trump, the poor often identify with the wealth and power of the rich. As a figure of excess, Trump represents the consumer object that is supposed to make up for everything we lack. From this perspective, consumerism gives us direct satisfaction of our drives without having to worry about the law, censorship, and desire of the Other.[44]

THE BOOB TUBE

Much of Trump's success has been driven by the news media, which no longer is focused on reporting the news but instead is centered on attracting the highest number of viewers so it can sell advertisements for the highest price or increase cable subscriptions. To understand this type of cultural environment where surplus value trumps all other values, we have to think of the new media news system as lacking any moral compass, and in the age of 24-hour multichannel news coverage, every station is so afraid of missing out on the big story that they tend to all present the same news as every other channel.[45] Here instead of the multiplicity of channels bringing a more diverse selection of information, everyone conforms to everyone else out of fear of missing out. Therefore, the obsessional narcissism of the liberal media results in an amoral viral circulation of sensationalist representations that caters to our unconscious desires and fears. In this system, someone like Trump gets much more coverage and exposure because he is always making news by saying unpredictable and outrageous things. Furthermore, since he combines conservative rhetoric with a manipulation of the liberal media, Trump reveals how liberals and conservatives actually function together.

In this neoliberal media culture, people from both political tendencies try to escape from any responsibility for what they say, and one way they do this is by feeding into the cultural opposition of criticism versus ignorant bliss. Within our entertainment culture, one seeks to enjoy without thinking, and the media delivers on this desire by presenting information so fast and so compacted that there is no time to break down and decode the messages being internalized. Instead of consciously examining social information in a critical way, fast media and fast talkers like Trump cater to unconscious processing. We can therefore think of the media as now playing the role of the gazing hypnotic fascist leader who is listened to by followers who have given up their critical faculties. Just as one stares into the gaze of the hypnotist who tells the hypnotized to ignore the world around her, the media watcher regresses to the primal masochistic relationship between the archaic father and the helpless child. The populism of the Left and the Right thus offer an infantilization of culture and politics.

BEYOND UNCONSCIOUS POPULISM

In the next chapter, I articulate a way out of the new populism on the Left and the Right, but first, I want to end by articulating how Trump's and Sanders' campaigns may be good for American politics and the rest of the world. As I have argued above, Trumps' free associations help to expose the underlying unconscious fantasies supporting the conservative coalition, and one effect of this discourse is that we are seeing the possible break-up of the Republican Party. Many of the elites in the conservative coalition reject Trump because he not only alienates many voters through his distasteful bullying, but he has also turned some of his aggression toward his own party. As a billionaire who can self-fund his run for the nomination, he reveals that the conservative push to allow for unlimited spending by individuals in campaigns can result in cutting out the party from the relationship between a candidate and a voter. Since he does not have to rely on the Republican Party for resources, he shows how money can lead to freedom, but in this case, it is freedom from the establishment.

In a similar way, Sanders has turned to individual small donors to bypass the Democratic Party, and in result of his efforts, the establishment has tried to counter his nomination through the use of super delegates and other party power plays. One possible result of this battle between Sanders and the Democratic establishment is that the party itself will be divided between a Left and a moderate wing. This division, in turn, could end up also destroying the Democrat Party at the same time the Republicans meet a similar fate. The question then becomes what happens when each party dissolves: will the people retreat into a state of total apathy or will they seek a new alternative. My argument in the next chapter will be that a real Left alternative has to emerge because the current form of politics is based on an investment in the nation state, which no longer can work in a globalized world. From a psychoanalytic perspective, the service provided by Trump and Sanders is that they have used a mode of free association to expose the repressed psychopathologies that have held together the Democratic and Republican coalitions.

NOTES

1. Freud, S. (1975). *Group psychology and the analysis of the ego*. New York: WW Norton & Company, p. 44.
2. Lacan, J. (1998). *The four fundamental concepts of psycho-analysis* (Vol. 11). New York: WW Norton & Company, p. 272.
3. Ibid., p. 273.
4. Ibid., p. 272.
5. Ibid.
6. Ibid.
7. Freud, *Group psychology*, p. 45.
8. Ibid., p. 39.
9. Ibid.
10. Ibid.
11. Lacan, *Four fundamental*, p. 275.
12. Freud, *Group psychology*, p. 47.
13. Ibid., p. 49.
14. Ibid.
15. Ibid., pp. 52–53.
16. Ibid., p. 52.
17. Ibid.
18. Ibid.
19. In Lacan's later works, he realizes that his original theory of Symbolic mediation represents an endorsement of linguistic and social alienation. He then argues that we need to find a way to separate from the Symbolic Other, who has no real actual existence but is defined by a set of social beliefs.
20. Ibid.
21. Ibid., p. 53.
22. For instance, Hobbes bases the need for the social contract on the fear of living in a state of natural war and anarchy.
23. Freud, *Group psychology*, p. 53.
24. Ibid., p. 54.
25. Ibid., pp. 54–55.
26. Ibid., p. 55.
27. Ibid.
28. Ibid., p. 56.
29. Ibid.
30. Freud posits that the sons are only able to overcome the primal father when they move from nonsexual identification with each other to homosexual object love, which has the result of freeing their libido so they have the ability to kill off the father (*Group psychology*, p. 56., note 1). From this perspective fascist groups have to repress homosexuality so that the homosocial bonding of the

followers can emerge. As Freud insists, the military and the church represent this same need to replace homosexuality with a nonsexual bond between the followers and with the leader.

31. Ibid., p. 57.
32. Ibid.
33. Ibid., p. 58.
34. Ibid., p. 57, notes, 1–2.
35. Ibid., p. 58.
36. Ibid., p. 59.
37. Eric Fromm's work often focuses on why people try to escape their own freedom by submitting themselves to the will of powerful others. Fromm, E. (1994). *Escape from freedom.* New York: Macmillan.
38. Felman, S., & Laub, D. (1992). *Testimony: Crises of witnessing in literature, psychoanalysis, and history.* New York: Taylor & Francis.
39. Žižek, *In defense of lost causes,* pp. 264–233.
40. Klein, N. (2015). *No logo.* Montreal: Éditions Actes Sud.
41. Freud, S., Strachey, J., & Freud, A. (1978). *Jokes and their relation to the unconscious.* London: Hogarth Press.
42. Achen, C. and Bartels, L. (2016, 23 May), Do Sanders supporters favor his policies? *The New York Times,* http://www.nytimes.com/2016/05/23/opinion/campaign-stops/do-sanders-supporters-favor-his-policies.html?_r=0.
43. Wilson, J.K. (1995). *The myth of political correctness: The conservative attack on higher education.* Raleigh: Duke University Press.
44. Miller, J.A. (2006). On shame. In J. Clemens, & R. Grigg (Eds.), *Jacques Lacan and the other side of psychoanalysis: reflections on Seminar XVII.* Raleigh: Duke University Press.
45. Fallows, J. (1997). *Breaking the news: How the media undermine American democracy. New York: Vintage.*

CHAPTER 5

Global Solidarity and Global Government: The Universal Subject of Psychoanalysis and Democracy

Abstract This chapter argues that we have to rethink the limits of nationalism as we recognize the need for a global government to confront the global challenges of climate change, financial capitalism, tax avoidance, terrorism, migration, and international poverty. By returning to the Freudian concepts of free association and the neutrality of the analyst, I offer a model for global solidarity and universal human rights.

Keywords Slavoj Zizek · Climate change · Global justice · Descartes · Universality · Global government · Naomi Klein · Freud · Lacan · Free association

My central argument is that if we want to overcome global problems like climate change, unfair trade, tax avoidance, and terrorism, we need to develop a global government and a new model of global solidarity. Psychoanalysis is important to this political project because this discourse helps us to think beyond nationalism and the capitalist death drive as we embrace a leap into universal justice. Following Descartes' promotion of universal democratic reason, I argue for a mode of subjectivity and solidarity that counters the political reliance on identification, idealization, projection, splitting, repression, the death drive, and empathy. This possibility of this form of global human rights is informed by the analytic connection between the neutrality of the analyst and the uncensored free associations of the patient.

© The Author(s) 2016

R. Samuels, *Psychoanalyzing the Left and Right After Donald Trump,*
Critical Theory and Practice in Psychology and the Human Sciences,
DOI 10.1007/978-3-319-44808-4_5

THE MORAL THIRD

As Jessica Benjamin has argued in relation to the Middle East conflict, a key to overcoming political antagonism is the establishment of what she calls a "moral third," which moves beyond "all of the basic oppositions of 'them and us' and 'doer and done-to' by recognizing that we all contain all opposites."[1] What she calls for is both a neutral view of conflict and the acknowledgement of all violations, sufferings, indignities, and debasements; in other words, she asks for a type of cultural psychoanalysis, where free association is used to affirm all aspects of the self and the Other without repression or denial. Yet, Benjamin also affirms that "our identification with the suffering of others can be interfered with by the identity of the victim..." (p. 7). In other words, one must find a way to transcend victim identity and victim identification as one continues to acknowledge the desires and abuses of the past. From a political and psychoanalytic perspective, we have to protect free speech and airing of personal and social grievances, but we also have to create a system of rights and laws that is universal and not based on the opposition between victims and persecutors.

For Benjamin, an important first step for overcoming victim politics and embracing social solidarity is to "move beyond self-interest to an identification with the Other..." (p. 8). Unfortunately, this now common call to identify with others as the key to social justice is called into question by psychoanalysis. As Lacan argued throughout his work, we have to ask who is this other with whom we are supposed to identify? While Benjamin appears to equate this other with other people who are different from us, Lacan posits that this Other represents the locus of language and the social.[2] Moreover, Lacan argues that when we identify with others, we create an Imaginary relationship of understanding that generates misrecognition and aggression.[3] Since we always see things from our own personal perspective, we tend to impose our beliefs and understandings onto others. A goal then of the analyst, according to Lacan, is to avoid being the Imaginary other by occupying the place of the Symbolic Other.[4] By affirming a position of neutrality, the analyst does not give in to the subject's demand for understanding, identification, idealization, or mirroring, and in the case of politics, this type of discourse requires positing a space for neutral laws and principles that can be universalized, and on the level of social movements, neutrality and universality demand a movement away from identity politics to a more global mode of coalition building around universal human rights.

Lacan's concept of the Other returns us to Descartes' notion that the key to modernity is the acceptance of the universality of reason. At the start of his *Discourse on Method*, he declares that, "Good sense is, of all things among men, the most equally distributed; for every one thinks himself so abundantly provided with it, that those even who are the most difficult to satisfy in everything else, do not usually desire a larger measure of this quality than they already possess. And in this it is not likely that all are mistaken; the conviction is rather to be held as testifying that the power of judging aright and of distinguishing truth from error, which is properly what is called good sense or reason, is by nature equal in all men."[5] Of course one could argue against Descartes and show how people do not have the same levels of reason, but that is not his point. His argument is based on a political principle that goes beyond experience and reason, and it is this leap into democracy that defines the subject of social solidarity. Democracy is then viewed as an impossible, but necessary, ideal that transcends individual desires and identifications.

As we saw in the previous chapter, Freud argued that the move toward Symbolic equality and social justice is predicated on overcoming Imaginary envy, rivalry, and jealousy. From this perspective, one accepts principles of universal justice because one does not want others to garner more attention or love. Here narcissistic self-interest reverses into the quest for social equality by replacing an Imaginary dual relationship with the other with a Symbolic relation with the universality of equality. It is vital to stress that this universal justice does not exist in nature or individual experience and thus requires a leap into the Symbolic.

Democracy and universal equality are therefore impossible ideals that we continue to pursue but cannot trace to any previous experience or perception. Furthermore, when Descartes turns to his development of the scientific method, he returns to this same unfounded principle in order to establish the ideals of objectivity and neutrality: "The first was never to accept anything for true which I did not clearly know to be such; that is to say, carefully to avoid precipitancy and prejudice, and to comprise nothing more in my judgment than what was presented to my mind so clearly and distinctly as to exclude all ground of doubt."[6] This move against prejudice is clearly an attempt to establish modern reason and science as a neutral perspective that counters the premodern emphasis on faith, fate, and belief. Once again, the leap into science represents an impossible ideal that has to be practiced as an artificial result of human language and sociality. Although one cannot be completely neutral or objective, the goal of analysis for Lacan is the training of analysts since the analyst has to learn how to recognize and suspend one's own prejudices. Of course, not everyone in analysis wants to become an analyst, but the goal is still to be able to take on the position of the analyst at the end of analysis. In terms of politics and social movements, an open self-critical discourse has to be maintained to constantly reveal and examine prejudices and unconscious passionate attachments.

One reason, therefore, why Lacan insists that psychoanalytic practice can only come into being after Descartes is that the neutrality of the analyst and the open mode of free association of the patient are both grounded on the impossible ideal of universal reason.[7] In both his practice and theories, Freud returned to this modern idea of reason, and yet it is important to point out that universality and science have been critiqued in postmodern times for failing to recognize difference and for imposing an abstract and alienating discourse.[8] However, Freud's practice is able to overcome these problems by combining the artificial neutrality of the analyst with the uncensored, unrestricted discourse of the patent.

As Lacan stresses, the neutrality of the analyst is essential in creating an artificial discourse where the analyst is able to represent society and language in general and not any particular Imaginary meaning or value.[9] This position of the analyst is necessary in order to avoid the pitfalls of idealization, identification, comprehension, and mirroring. Since the analyst refuses to satisfy the demands of the patient, and the fundamental rule calls for the patient to speak without thinking about what the social Other thinks, analysis provides a space for the patient to encounter all aspects of the self through language without repression and denial. Thus, in opposition to Benjamin's call for the subject to identify with the other in order to create a third space for political reconciliation, Lacan argues that the analyst must desire only the continuation of free association.[10] Instead of feeding the mirroring and idealizing transference that we find in analysts like Kohut, Lacan shows the dangers in creating the illusion of empathy and understanding.

UNIVERSALITY AND THE NEED FOR GLOBAL GOVERNMENT

The first step, then, in overcoming global problems like climate change is to establish the leap into democratic universality beyond calls for identity and identification. This artificial production of the universal subject of reason has to be connected to a discourse of speech that refuses self-censorship and the need to be recognized by the other. As we shall see in analyzing Naomi Klein's *This Changes Everything*, the only way to deal with global climate change is through the creation of a global government, but we shall see that our investment in nationalistic identities and identifications blocks this possibility. Moreover, as Klein argues, neoliberal politics and consumer culture feed the destruction of our environment; however, what she is unable to confront is the way that human action is shaped by an unacknowledged drive. Psychoanalysis is therefore necessary to for us to think beyond nationalism, neoliberalism, and global self-destruction.

One of Klein's main arguments is that the only way we can overcome the challenges caused by climate change is if we develop a new model of global social solidarity: "For any of this to change, a worldview will need to rise to the fore that sees nature, other nations, and our own neighbors not as adversaries, but rather as partners in a grand project of mutual reinvention."[11] Since we share the same climate and environment, we have to move beyond our current system of nation states and national identifications, and yet Klein does not make a call for a global form of government. One reason for her blind spot on this issue is that even such a radical thinker is locked into the ideology of nationalism, and so we must ask, what does psychoanalysis tells us about our investment in national identities?

As Benedict Anderson has stressed, nation states are Imaginary entities built out of social negotiations, but the power of these Imaginary bodies is hard to resist.[12] From Lacan's perspective, one reason why it is difficult to overcome Imaginary constructions is that our identities and identifications are build out of a narcissistic and defensive relationship to the world.[13] Just as we seek to defend the unity and integrity of our bodies, we also seek to defend the integrity of our knowledge and our identifications. Since, according to Lacan, the very possibility of an ego is formed in a mirroring and idealizing identification, we can consider the Imaginary borders of a nation to be an extension of the self that has to be defended at all costs. Thus, even in an age of multinational corporations and globalization, people cling to their national identities.

For Zizek, one defining aspect of modern nationalism is the conflict between the universalizing nature of capitalism and the primal fixation on ethnic identity.[14] As Marx claimed, capitalism spreads throughout the world and does not respect national boundaries, and so it upsets all ethnic traditions and religious foundations. Nationalism is then a way of recentering the world that has been decentered by the heedless, headless drive of universalizing capital. Zizek adds that as our world becomes more global and interconnected through trade, travel, and the Internet, the desire for ethnic and national identity only increases.[15] Moreover, he claims that all of the attempts to create a global democracy fail because they cannot overcome the pathology of nationalism and nation-state.

Zizek uses the model of the formation of a neurotic symptom as the foundation for his understanding of our investments in nationalism. In this structure, ethnic identity represents the primary fixation that is repressed by universal democracy and capitalist exchange value and then returns in the form of nationalist movements.[16] From Zizek's dialectical perspective, what makes the universality of modernity possible in the first place is that it is reliant on an exception in the form of the national cause: "[T]he national Cause is ultimately the way subjects of a given nation organize their collective enjoyment through national myths."[17] Something, then, that blocks the possibility of a global government is that this universal system does not provide people with the unconscious enjoyment that they derive from being part of a particular national group. Moreover, Zizek explains xenophobia as driven by people's fear that other cultures and immigrants are trying to steal away their particular mode of ethnic enjoyment.[18]

This question of what to do about our investment in national and ethnic identities can be related to Lacan's critique of Descartes and modernity. In his *The Four Fundamental Concepts of Psychoanalysis*, Lacan argues that Descartes can teach us much about how transference works and the limits of modern reason because at the very moment Descartes bases reason on universal doubt, he cannot help but turn toward a god as the final guarantee for all truth.[19] Here we see how modernity was never able to fully dissociate itself from premodern religion, and that the more one attempts to expose all certainties to reason and doubt, the more one ends up relying on an idealized Other who is supposed to be the one who knows. In short, modernity never went far enough in its critique of religion and nationalism because of the need for an idealized moral order and a stable body of knowledge in the face of the growing power of universal doubt and capitalistic destabilization.

Nationalism and fundamentalist religious movements can therefore be considered to be the symptoms of globalized capitalism, science, and democracy. Just as individuals can never fully escape their primal sexual investments, the attempt to move to a global government will always be haunted by a primal investment in religion, ethnicity, and the nation-state. However, psychoanalysis is dedicated to working through the transference and repressed fixations, and here we see a major limitation in Zizek's work. He simply does not focus on transference, free association, and the practice of analytic treatment, and so all he can do is describe social symptoms without positing any real alternatives.[20] In fact, Zizek rejects the possibility of a neutral space for law and universal justice, and so it is hard to imagine how he could affirm universal subjectivity and global human rights.[21]

A psychoanalytic politics would have to use the neutrality of the analyst and the open discourse of free association to work through our investments in fantasies and cultural enjoyments, and this requires exposing the unconscious investments in religion, ethnicity, and nationalism. Part of this process will require eliminating the forces that drive people to premodern authority, and this means establishing a global guaranteed income and a global wealth tax. If economic insecurity pushes people into the arms of nationalistic and religious fundamentalism, the only real solution is to counter the way capitalism destabilizes the lives of billions of people around the world. In short, there can be no universal justice or democracy if we hold onto the ethnic Thing or the idealized religious Other, and people will only give up their passionate attachments if they are no longer needed to stabilize their lives. This also means that autocratic leaders relying on nationalism and religion to control their people have to be exposed and countered. Modernity is thus an unfinished project that has failed to fully articulate an alternative to the premodern order.

Modern Science vs. Scientism

Like many critics of modernity and science, Naomi Klein does not take on nationalism, and instead, she focuses on how capitalism and science are founded on alienating and destructive principles: "I have also come to understand, over the course of researching this book, that the shift will require rethinking the very nature of humanity's power—our right to extract ever more without facing consequences, our capacity to bend complex natural systems to our will. This is a shift that challenges not only capitalism, but also the building blocks of materialism that preceded modern capitalism..."[22] Klein here repeats a common postmodern criticism of modern science and capitalism, and this concerns the way that the modern mindset sees nature and other people as raw material that have to be mastered and utilized for social purposes.[23] However, from a psychoanalytic viewpoint, it is important at this point to differentiate between modern science and scientism. In thinkers like Descartes and Freud, we can think of science as the intellectual discovery of truth through the use of artificial structures (math). From this perspective, science represents the pure pursuit of truth for truth's sake, and is therefore equivalent to the process of free association. On the other hand, scientism is an ideology that claims to know and master the Real from a perspective of ideal knowledge.[24] For example, current theories of neuroscience and evolutionary psychology tend to argue that all of our mental disturbances are caused by our genes, which have been selected through evolution. These neoliberal "sciences" represent a total version of scientism that does not allow for the free discovery of truth.[25] Furthermore, this perspective of scientism sees nature and other people as simply usable products for its already-established theories and interpretations.

In the case of psychoanalysis, scientism is challenged because the patient is told to pursue whatever comes to mind without intention or censoring, and the analyst is not supposed to direct the flow of discovery.[26] This mode of free speech eventually encounters the fact that not everything can be symbolized, and so there is a limit to language and discourse. In fact, Lacan argues that the analyst embodies this limit to language, and that one of the things that disrupt the quest for total knowledge and understanding is that the analyst refuses to be viewed by the patient and respond to the patient's requests for satisfaction, love, and understanding.[27] The analyst then frustrates the demand for an idealized Other, and in this way, analysis helps to move beyond religion and scientism.

In terms of capitalism, we also need to distinguish between the artificial system of exchange values and the compulsive investment in the headless, heedless drive for acquisition and satisfaction. Since in analysis, there is no direct satisfaction of the drives by the patient or the analyst, one is forced to encounter the impossible desires that move the psyche and which capitalistic drives seek to satisfy. As Lacan was fond of repeating, psychoanalysis for Freud was not about liberating sexuality; rather, analysis produces a controlled experience of the encounter with the dissatisfaction of desire.[28] Since desire is always a desire for what one does not have, there is no possibility of ultimately fulfilling our desire, and yet we compulsively try to satisfy our drives.

A psychoanalytic politics has to recognize the role that transference, desire, and drives play in capitalism and science, but we have to be careful not to simply demonizing these modern endeavors. After all, as I stated above, modern universality is a key to global solidarity; however, the problem is that the project of modernity itself never went far enough because it did not take on religion, nationalism, scientism, and compulsive capitalism. The question then is can we have a global representative democracy that is able to shed its reliance on premodern ideologies?

BEYOND BINARY THINKING

Returning to Klein's text, we find that instead of embracing the principle of universal human rights and the suspension of victim fantasies, we encounter a binary logic that pits the need for collective action to fight climate change against conservative political interests: "It requires heavy-duty interventions: sweeping bans on polluting activities, deep subsidies for green alternatives, pricey penalties for violations, new taxes, new public works programs, reversals of privatizations—the conservatives' list of ideological outrages goes on and on. Everything, in short, that these think tanks—which have always been public proxies for far more powerful corporate interests—have been busily attacking..."[29] Of course, it would be hard to argue against Klein's focus on the conservative attempt to discredit climate change science and the need for collective action and governmental intervention, but we have to ask what is the effect of relying on an analysis that clearly separates the world between good liberals and bad conservatives?

Psychoanalysis tells us that the Left's need to demonize the Right often comes at the cost of blaming all problems on an outside group, while the liberal subject remains a blameless victim. The problem is that in the case of climate change, we are all perpetrators and victims, and very little will change if liberals hold onto their fantasies of innocence and purity. On one level, Klein does recognize that this global problem requires a universal principle of justice, but on another level, her rhetoric relies on a clear distinction between the good self and the hated other: "Even climate action at home looks suspiciously like socialism to them; all the calls for high-density affordable housing and brand-new public transit are obviously just ways to give backdoor subsidies to the undeserving poor. Never mind what this war on carbon means to the very premise of global free trade, with its insistence that geographical distance is a mere fiction to be collapsed by Walmart's diesel trucks and Maersk's container ships."[30] This constant invoking of a binary separation of good and bad actors goes against the psychoanalytic call to use free association to confront the good and bad aspects of our selves and of others. The question remains of how we can break out of this battle of ideologies that relies on both sides defining themselves against the other side. My point here is that we should not simply dismiss the destructive actions of the conservative coalition; however, we have to affirm a break with these dueling ideologies in order to affirm the universality of the global subject.

Since we all participate in the global system of scientific and capitalistic exploitation of nature, the effort to blame a clear target for all of our problems places liberals in the position of the innocent victim or the "beautiful soul" that sees disorder only coming from the outside. Thus, the obsessional narcissist's need to see itself as all good blocks the awareness of how we are all part of the problem, and therefore we all have to be part of the solution. For example, in the following passage, Klein's focus on corporations and wealthy nations as the cause of our problem shields us from seeing how we are all invested in the unstoppable capitalistic drive: "The corporate quest for natural resources will become more rapacious, more violent. Arable land in Africa will continue to be seized to provide food and fuel to wealthier nations, unleashing a new stage of neocolonial plunder layered on top of the most plundered places on Earth."[31] Of course, it is our desire for consumer goods that feeds neocolonial capitalism, but because Klein relies on a clear distinction between victim and perpetrator, she reinforces the splitting of the subject and the other into all-good and all-bad parts, and this splitting makes any reconciliation impossible because both sides will take comfort in their purified victim status.

At times, Klein does realize that since climate change affects everyone, it opens the door for a universal perspective, but she still finds it necessary to focus on the political divide between bad conservatives and good liberals: "For a long time, environmentalists spoke of climate change as a great equalizer, the one issue that affected everyone, rich or poor. It was supposed to bring us together. Yet all signs are that it is doing precisely the opposite, stratifying us further into a society of haves and have-nots, divided between those whose wealth offers them a not insignificant measure of protection from ferocious weather, at least for now, and those left to the mercy of increasingly dysfunctional states."[32] Of course, Klein is right to see how people will be victimized by climate change in different ways according to their wealth and power, and yet her need to depict clear winners and losers undermines her ability to call for global solidarity and the need for a global government to enforce universal laws and principles. After all, if we destroy our world, not even the rich will survive.

THE LEAP INTO UNIVERSALITY

In connecting the universal subject of democracy to the neutrality of the psychoanalyst and the free associations of the patient, I have been arguing that the way to both recognize injustice and move beyond it is to leap into an unnatural discourse of universal human rights. To help clarify what I mean by this structure, I will reflect on my experience as being a union president, since one of the things a union has to do is to insist on the same rights and practices for all people. For example, I have often had to defend people who I do not like or who are against unions. My defense of their right to due process has nothing to do with empathy or a judgment on their innocence or guilt; rather, a universal right to due process bypasses the need for an individual judgment of value. This move toward universality and away from empathy is a key to establishing global solidarity and justice because other models of political judgment rely on subjective determinations of value. For instance, in the case of empathy, people have to make a determination of whether someone is worthy of attention, or if someone is really innocent, and these judgments are often shaped by political and personal views.[33]

While many recent academic thinkers and psychologists have argued that empathy is the key to promoting social justice, I am arguing here that from a psychoanalytic perspective, the analyst suspends empathy and judgment in order to allow for the free flow of discourse and discovery from a universal, neutral perspective. Instead of pretending to be the one who knows all of the answers or the one who can save the patient, Freud stressed that the analyst must allow patients to discover the truth on their own because they will only really be convinced if it comes from their own discourse, and it is essential to help the patient become more independent and less reliant on an idealized authority figure. Moreover, since the analyst does not judge the patient, the subject can explore both the good and bad aspects of the self and the other.

Many critics have argued that this stress on the independence of the subject feeds an ideology of individualism that undermines any possibility of collective action or social solidarity.[34] However, we have to look at how new social movements are being formed and maintained. Instead of the old Marxist idea that there is a single class of people who must lead a revolution and that revolution is determined by a single theory of history, post-Marxist social movements function through the building of coalitions focused on the idea that people make history, and there is no preordained path or leader.[35] Moreover, coalition politics rely on united groups with radically different identities and interests around a common set of causes. In fact, Klein points to this new theory of social movements when she describes a growing movement for global social justice: "And most of all, it means continually drawing connections among these seemingly disparate struggles—asserting, for instance, that the logic that would cut pensions, food stamps, and health care before increasing taxes on the rich is the same logic that would blast the bedrock of the earth to get the last vapors of gas and the last drops of oil before making the shift to renewable energy."[36] By linking different struggles together, a broader and stronger social movement can be made, but one quickly runs into the problem of identity politics, and this is where psychoanalysis can help out.

Instead of basing social movements on the need for each group to recognize the suffering and identity of the other groups, the subject of psychoanalysis moves beyond the desire for recognition and judgment. This does not mean that injustices and past harms are simply repressed or denied; rather, the coalition realizes that its strength relies on universal principles and rights that transcend particular identities and histories. Although, this sounds a lot like the idea of colorblind justice, a key difference is that free association supports the right to air grievances, but it does not base its principles and rights on victim identity and identification. On the one hand, there is a recognition of injustice, yet on the other hand, the push is for inclusive principles of justice from the perspective of a neutral third party.

For Zizek, the push for pure universality can never be attained because it always relies on an exception or remainder in the form of a pathological investment in the nation-state or ethnic identity.[37] Zizek argues that the possibility of formal democracy and universality is generated out of the pathological exception, and therefore, there is no way to escape from identity politics, nationalism, and fundamentalism. However, I have been arguing that Descartes' democratic subject and the process of psychoanalysis both offer an alternative to Zizek's theory. For instance, while

Zizek dismisses the notion that disputes can be decided from a neutral perspective, psychoanalysis is centered on promoting the impossible, but necessary ideal of neutrality. As Laclau effectively argues, Zizek also does not propose any real alternative to our current neoliberal status quo.[38]

THE LIBERAL HATRED OF CAPITALISM

For Klein and many critics on the radical Left, there can be no neutrality because the clear enemy of our society is unregulated capitalism and science: "[T]he real reason we are failing to rise to the climate moment is because the actions required directly challenge our reigning economic paradigm (deregulated capitalism combined with public austerity), the stories on which Western cultures are founded (that we stand apart from nature and can outsmart its limits), as well as many of the activities that form our identities and define our communities (shopping, living virtually, shopping some more)."[39] From this perspective, modern science combined with consumer capitalism is the clear cause for the destruction of our climate. Since capitalism activates our drives and fantasies, it gives us access to the passionate attachments that Zizek argues prevents us from affirming the empty universality of the democratic subject.[40] For Zizek, fantasies are the particular modes of enjoyment that we hide from others; moreover, fantasies provide an Imaginary solution to the conflict between civilization and individual desire, and the neoliberal ideology of consumer capitalism represents the social foundation for absorbing the social economic system into a personal experience.

Zizek affirms that psychoanalysis works by exposing fantasies and allowing individuals to assume some kind of distance from their own pathological investments. In terms of political discourse, we can see how Trump's desire to "make America great again," exposes the nationalistic investment in exceptionalism. For example, his call to use stronger methods of torture than waterboarding goes against international law and reveals how Americans do not want to play by the same rules and laws as everyone else. When crowds cheer for Trump's endorsement of the need to stop being politically correct and embrace torture, they help to surface the passionate attachments and sadistic fantasies that support imperialism and nationalism. These calls have to be publically condemned, but liberals should not pretend that they do not also participate in nationalistic exceptionalism.

One of the clearest ways that liberal politicians have fueled religion, nationalism, and fundamentalism is through the support of oppressive autocratic regimes. For instance, when Hillary Clinton was Secretary of State, she approved huge arms deals to the most oppressive Islamic states at the same time she promoted the protection of women's rights and global human rights. Moreover, the Clinton Foundation received large contributions from Saudi Arabia and other autocratic countries in the Middle East right before Secretary Clinton approved of arms deals for these same countries.[41] Therefore, at the same time that Clinton was fighting terrorism and the Islamic attack on women's rights, she helped to arm and support the nations who were exporting terror and subjecting their own populace to extreme forms of sexist oppression. This liberal hypocrisy is just part of a long history of wealthy Western nations supporting oppressive regimes around the world for their own economic benefit or perceived nationalist interests.

THE NEED FOR GLOBAL GOVERNMENT

I have been arguing that in order to overcome problems like terrorism, theocracy, and climate change, we need a global government, which requires an overcoming of nationalism, and as Klein shows, the only way to fight inequality and poverty is to counter the current form of global free trade: "But in the past, when workers organized to demand better wages, and when city dwellers organized to demand cleaner air, the companies were pretty much forced to improve both working and environmental standards. That changed with the advent of free trade: thanks to the removal of virtually all barriers to capital flows, corporations could pick up and leave every time labor costs started rising."[42] Since multinational corporations can go anywhere in the world to escape labor and environmental laws and restrictions, there needs to be a global form of government that can enforce universal standards; however, Klein always falls short of calling for a global government that would be able to write and regulate global trade. In other words, she maintains an unstated commitment to the current political order of nation-states, and even if she endorses better international trade deals, these arrangements are structured by the interests of particular nations.

From a liberal-progressive perspective, Klein shows what we need to do to fight climate change and global poverty, but her commitment to the current world order prevents her from making the call for a new global order: "Unlike encouraging energy efficiency, the measures we must take to secure a just, equitable, and inspiring transition away from fossil fuels clash directly with our reigning economic orthodoxy at every level. As we will see, such a shift breaks all the ideological rules—it requires visionary long-term planning, tough regulation of business, higher levels of taxation for the affluent, big public sector expenditure, and in many cases reversals of core privatizations in order to give communities the power to make the changes they desire. In short, it means changing everything about how we think about the economy..."[43] As we see here, the focus on economics prevents a clear global solution because there is no articulation of what international institutions have to be created in order to enforce a different economic order. Furthermore, by blaming capitalism and conservative politics for all of the world's problems, Klein is blind to the force of nationalism, victim identification, and liberal moralism.

Klein's failure to call for a global government is tied to her inability to think of the global democratic subject as a set of universal principles beyond any particular identity or identification. Each time that she approaches this need for the leap into democratic universality, she falls back into a divisive discourse of clear victims and perpetrators: "The lesson from all this is not that people won't sacrifice in the face of the climate crisis. It's that they have had it with our culture of lopsided sacrifice, in which individuals are asked to pay higher prices for supposedly green choices while large corporations dodge regulation and not only refuse to change their behavior, but charge ahead with ever more polluting activities."[44] The underlying fatalism of the Left is exposed here as we see that evil capitalism is opposed to the blameless victims-citizens.[45]

One way that the Left is able to criticize the entire capitalist and scientific system, while remaining removed from any responsibility, is by turning to historical narratives that privilege social forces over individual subjectivity. For instance, in Klein's description of modern science, capitalism, and imperialism, she does not examine what unconscious forces drive people to exploit nature, others, and themselves: "These ideas of a completely knowable and controllable earth animated not only the Scientific Revolution but, critically, the colonial project as well, which sent ships crisscrossing the globe to poke and prod and bring the secrets, and wealth, back to their respective crowns. The mood of human invincibility that governed this epoch was neatly encapsulated in the words of clergyman and philosopher William Derham in his 1713 book *Physico-Theology*: 'We can, if need be, ransack the whole globe, penetrate into the bowels of the earth, descend to the bottom of the deep, travel to the farthest regions.'"[46] The question that this passage forces us to ask is what aspects of human psychology allows for unlimited greed and the exploitation of others? What is then missing from this populism of the Left is the role played by drives as a form of internalized self-destruction and self-hatred.

THE CAPITALIST DEATH DRIVE

One of Freud's key insights was that people willingly participate in their own self-destruction. In what he eventually called the death drive, Freud realized that people have an unconscious sense of guilt, anxiety, and the need for punishment, and at the same time, they engage in compulsive, self-destructive activities to efface their guilt and anxiety.[47] Through his theory of moral masochism, Freud highlighted how the initial relationship between the helpless child and the all-powerful parent creates a fundamental fantasy that equates love with the need to be punished. This fantasy then is taken up by the death drive as people find enjoyment in their own self-destruction.[48] For example, addicts turn to a specific object or drug in order to control their anxiety, but they soon become dependent on their method of escape, and they lose their control over their solution. In the case of consumer capitalism, people engage in compulsive buying as a way of reducing anxiety through the illusion of control over an object or social relationship, yet, they soon realize that they cannot control themselves and cannot stop consuming.

What Freud discovered is that for the human subject, anything can be sexualized, including pain and self-destruction. Capitalism, then, takes advantage of the sexual drives by providing opportunities for compulsive behavior. Just as Marx argued that the spread of capitalism is an unstoppable force spreading around the globe and overcoming all solid traditions and borders, Freud realized that sexuality can spread to all parts of the human anatomy and all aspects of human thought. For example, I once had a patient who was addicted to buying shoes and unsafe sex; in the case of both compulsions, he reported that he received extreme enjoyment from these activities, and they offered him a way of escaping from his miserable life. However, after he engaged in these activities, he always felt guilty and ashamed, and this created an anxiety that could only be alleviated by more compulsive activities. Therefore, he sought to escape his own guilt and anxiety by losing himself in activities he could not control.

Compulsive consuming can thus free us from guilt, shame, and anxiety, but it also instills a profound alienation and opens the door for self-effacement. Likewise, Marx showed how capitalism can free us from premodern traditions and hierarchies, but we also are subjected to the headless, heedless drive for accumulation and expansion. The task, then, for a psychoanalytic politics of global social justice is to determine how to utilize the universalizing aspects of language and capitalism to promote the universal subject of democracy without the "enjoyment" of self-destruction. In other words, how do we break the bonds of the superego that feeds off of the primal relation between the powerful parent and the helpless child, which links law to punishment, guilt, and enjoyment?

This psychoanalytic theory of the death drives helps us to imagine a form of capitalism that would not be self-destructive and compulsive, but this would require a social process where capitalism is no longer experienced as an addictive way to overcome anxiety, loss, and guilt. Part of this social process would be to stabilize economic inequality through a global wealth tax and a universal basic income. After all, one of the things that turn capitalism into a self-destructive drive is the way that it produces both excess and lack; people consume in order to chase after the objects that will fill their lacking lives, but their lives are often lacking because they compare their wealth to others, and no one ever has enough money. The only way to reduce this problem is to find a more just and equitable way of reducing inequality around the world. Of course, desire and inequality will never be completely eliminated, but we have to find ways to reduce the ability of capitalism to shape people's lives.

Unfortunately, instead of clearly connecting the internal mechanisms of subjectivity like the death drive to external social formations, postmodern thinkers and activists have often focused on how universality and equal rights are always based on eliminating certain groups from consideration.[49] For instance, the universal claim that "All men are created equal," has been used to exclude noncitizens, women, slaves, people of color, and people without property. From the postmodern perspective, social movements are centered on including the excluded groups into the universal, but the postmodern academic approach to this problem has been to stress that every universal actually represents the vested interests of particular groups, and thus there can be no universals at all. Moreover, the quest for universal human rights always runs into the problem of dealing with cultural differences and the desire to protect particular ethnic and national practices and beliefs.

Global social justice and the fight against climate change therefore require a modern model of Symbolic ideals because universal principles are not based on material reality or natural order. On a fundamental social and subjective level, universal idealism represents a break with any conception of human nature or historical determinism: as we find in the position of the analyst in psychoanalysis, we need to cling to the impossible but necessary role of neutrality as we suspend the desire for moral judgment and empathic understanding. Although passionate attachments have to be exposed, we need to establish a space for a global universal order of rights and principles.

THE DECLARATION OF UNIVERSAL HUMAN RIGHTS

I argue that we can find a foundation for the move to universal human rights and a system of global principles in the United Nation's Universal Declaration of Human Rights.[50] This universalizing constitution combines together the open respect for cultural difference and individual freedom with universal principles of justice. What we now require is a global government to enforce these rights, and this requires powerful nations to give up their independent military and policing operations in favor of a global force.

The Preamble of the Universal Declaration of Human Rights begins by making the following universalizing claim: "Whereas recognition of the inherent dignity and of the equal and inalienable rights of all members of the human family is the foundation of freedom, justice and peace in the world." The first move is to reimagine the family as the human race, which demands an inherent dignity protected by equal and inalienable rights. From Laclau's perspective, "dignity," "Freedom," "justice," and "peace" might be considered to be empty signifiers and impossible demands; however, the selection of these should not be taken as a purely content-free gesture.[51] The universal principles and values are impossible ideals, but they structure a whole host of laws, institutions, and social movements. Just as in the case of psychoanalysis, the analyst can never be purely neutral, the idea is that we must strive to attain principles that are inherently unattainable, and this failure for full completion is what drives the desire for a more perfect universality.

The trick then in the Declaration and the potential global government is to balance universal neutrality with particular judgments, which can be universalized. For instance, in the continuation of the Preamble, universal rights are approached through their negation: "Whereas disregard and contempt for human rights have resulted in barbarous acts which have outraged the conscience of mankind, and the advent of a world in which human beings shall enjoy freedom of speech and belief and freedom from fear and want has been proclaimed as the highest aspiration of the common people." Once again, it is hard to imagine how people will ever be without want, but that is why it is posited as an aspiration; from a psychoanalytic perspective, the unconditional demand for love and recognition will never be completely fulfilled, but the lack of fulfillment fuels desire and propels the subject forward. Although the world will never be without want, we can locate here a fundamental desire to reduce the lack of basic material needs. Furthermore, the passage cited above begins by recognizing that the world is not inherently good, and people and nations do commit horrible acts, and so it is necessary to combine the pursuit of universal principles with free speech and open discourse so that the failures of the ideal can be recognized.

This recognition of barbarity in civilization is coupled with a realization that the failure of law and universal human rights results in rebellion, tyranny, oppression, and war between nations: "Whereas it is essential, if man is not to be compelled to have recourse, as a last resort, to rebellion against tyranny and oppression, that human rights should be protected by the rule of law; Whereas it is essential to promote the development of friendly relations between nations." Here we see one of the limitations off this document since the UN is still focused on the relation between nations, and therefore, it does not combine universal rights with a global government. What the Declaration promotes is that individual nations adopt universal standards, principles, and rights: "Human Rights as a common standard of achievement for all peoples and all nations, to the end that every individual and every organ of society, keeping this Declaration constantly in mind, shall strive by teaching and education to promote respect for these rights and freedoms and by progressive measures, national and international, to secure their universal and effective recognition and observance, both among the peoples of Member States themselves and among the peoples of territories under their jurisdiction." What is then missing from the Declaration and the United Nations itself is any real way of enforcing the principles it advocates. In short, without a global government and enforcement mechanism, the rights can be easily ignored. Of course, it is this needed consolidation of global power and violence that scares people and makes them cling to their national monopolies of violence.

One question to ask is what would it mean if there was a global representative democracy with its own police and military force? Would this type of monopolization of the use of force break the current cycle of state-sponsored war and terrorism? To begin to answer these questions, we have to look at the core principles of the Declaration. For instance, following Descartes, the first Article does call for a leap into democratic universality: "All human beings are born free and equal in dignity and rights. They are endowed with reason and conscience and should act towards one another in a spirit of brotherhood." Like Descartes, the first move is to affirm the impossible ideal of equal reason, which is then tied to the notion that everyone is born in a state of freedom and equal rights and dignity. Once again, it should be clear that none of these claims are actually true, and so they must represent impossible but necessary, ideals.

One reason why the principles have to remain open and transcendent is that the list of needed protected categories continues to expand. For example, Article 2 points to the growing number of identity groups seeking protected status: "Everyone is entitled to all the rights and freedoms set forth in this Declaration, without distinction of any kind, such as race, colour, sex, language, religion, political or other opinion, national or social origin, property, birth or other status. Furthermore, no distinction shall be made on the basis of the political, jurisdictional or international status of the country or territory to which a person belongs, whether it be independent, trust, non-self-governing or under any other limitation of sovereignty." Here we find a great example of the dialectical nature of human rights: the universal is continually expanded through the inclusion of previously excluded particular categories. Furthermore, the universality of these rights renders problematic the ability of any particular nation to have specific laws; in short, the nation state cannot sustain the universality of human rights. It is also vital to recognize that identity politics still plays an important role in expanding universal rights, but the key is that no single demographic group is able to dominate the process, and each group is able to demand inclusion without excluding other groups.

Article 6 also challenges the existence of nations since it requires equal protection by the law on a global scale: "Everyone has the right to recognition everywhere as a person before the law." This principle excludes exceptions, such as the U.S.'s attempt to determine which international laws apply to its national interests; from this perspective, there is no American exceptionalism, and so national laws have to be transcended. Since it is rare that Western developed nations engage in civil wars, the hope is that the formation of a global state will dramatically reduce warfare, and in this structure, terrorism would be treated as an internal matter of policing. In other words, terrorism would be depoliticized and undermined through the process of global solidarity.

The Declaration also calls into question religious laws and restrictions: "Men and women of full age, without any limitation due to race, nationality or religion, have the right to marry and to found a family. They are entitled to equal rights as to marriage, during marriage and at its dissolution." Clearly many Islamic states would have a great problem with this principle and several other articles, and so we are left with the difficult question of what to do about ethnic and national practices that counter the universality of these human rights. In fact, Article 18 tries to deal specifically with this conflict between religion and modern universality: "Everyone has the right to freedom of thought, conscience and religion; this right includes freedom to change his religion or belief, and freedom, either alone or in community with others and in public or private, to manifest his religion or belief in teaching, practice, worship and observance." Like the U.S. constitution, the proposed solution to the conflict between universality and particular religious beliefs is to protect the freedom of religion, but what remains unclear is what to do when particular religious practices conflict with universal human rights. According to the overall structure of the Declaration, particular ethnic and religious practices should be respected and protected unless they go against generalized rights, and in the case of this conflict, the universal always takes precedence over the particular.

In terms of economics, the Declaration offers a set of ideal principles that can only be realized through a very different global system: "Everyone has the right to work, to free choice of employment, to just and favourable conditions of work and to protection against unemployment. Everyone, without any discrimination, has the right to equal pay for equal work. Everyone who works has the right to just and favourable remuneration ensuring for himself and his family an existence worthy of human dignity, and supplemented, if necessary, by other means of social protection. Everyone has the right to form and to joint trade unions for the protection of his interests." These economic principles represent a global welfare state that would protect workers through unionization and basic employment rights. Ultimately the idea is to eliminate union-free zones and states and nations where workers' rights are not protected. However, the limitation of this set of principles is that does not go the next step and call for the public ownership of utilities and other vital services. Furthermore, it is hard to imagine how to protect the dignity and security of the worker without a form of global socialism.

Another limitation of the Declaration is that it only makes lower education free and universal and returns to the ideology of meritocracy in terms of higher education: "Everyone has the right to education. Education shall be free, at least in the elementary and fundamental stages. Elementary education shall be compulsory. Technical and professional education shall be made generally available and higher education shall be equally accessible to all on the basis of merit." As we have seen in the United States, this focus on merit would result in the production of inequality and the limitation of social mobility. Yet, at the same moment the Declaration falls back into a unequal discourse of unequal meritocracy, it also promotes an expansive model for education in general: "Education shall be directed to the full development of the human personality and to the strengthening of respect for human rights and fundamental freedoms. It shall promote understanding, tolerance and friendship among all nations, racial or religious groups, and shall further the activities of the United Nations for the maintenance of peace." Here education is tied to the training for global citizenship and the promotion of human development and not simply preparation for the job market.

It is vital to emphasize that all of these wonderful sounding universal rights can only be protected if there are global institutions that can enforce them. Article 28 makes a claim in this direction: "Everyone is entitled to a social and international order in which the rights and freedoms set forth in this Declaration can be fully realized." The problem with this call for an international order strong enough to protect these universal principles and rights is that it does not exist, and the Declaration does not provide a roadmap for how a system of global law can be instituted.

Not only do we need a global system of law to protect human rights, but we also need a global system of rules and enforcement to establish a fair system of taxation and labor regulations. In the current international order, multinational corporations have the ability to escape taxation and minimum wage rules by moving their profits and operations to locations that have very low tax rates and minimal labor laws.[52] Moreover, nations like the United States help to impoverish African nations by subsidizing American agriculture, while China undercuts global prices through currency manipulation. The only way, then, to deal with global poverty is to have global rules and laws enforced by a global system of justice and a single world currency. However, currently, powerful corporations and nations are able to control international laws through the creation of "free" trade deals that often work against social and economic justice. Furthermore, the power of selected nations to veto United Nation's resolutions undermines the ability of the UN to impose global law and principles.

Moving to the type of global government I am calling for here will not be easy or inevitable, but it is the only possible solution to our global problems. As a counter to the virtually unregulated movement of multinational capitalism, we need a global social justice movement that suspends particular passions and identifications in favor of universal solidarity and the commitment to universal principles and human rights. This effort will require collective action and organization coupled with education dedicated to democratic processes, and this call for democracy has to be combined with a psychoanalytic notion of universal subjectivity.

NOTES

1. Benjamin, J. (2015). Non-violence as respect for all suffering: Thoughts inspired by Eyad El Sarraj. *Psychoanalysis, Culture & Society, 21*(1), 7.
2. Lacan, J., Miller, J.A., & Forrester, J. (1988). *The seminar of Jacques Lacan. Book 2, The ego in Freud's theory and in the technique of psychoanalysis, 1954–1955.* New York: Norton, pp. 244–246.
3. Lacan, J. (1977). The mirror stage as formative of the function of the I as revealed in psychoanalytic experience. In *Ecrits: A selection.* New York: Norton.
4. Lacan articulates this notion that the analyst must represent the Symbolic Other in his early work. See Lacan, J., Miller, J.A., & Forrester, J. (1988). *The seminar of Jacques Lacan. Book 2, The ego in Freud's theory and in the technique of psychoanalysis, 1954–1955.* New York: Norton, p. 324.
5. Descartes, R., & Sutcliffe, F. (1968). *Discourse on method and the meditations.* London: Penguin UK, p. 1.
6. Ibid., p. 6.
7. Lacan, J. (1998). *The four fundamental concepts of psycho-analysis* (Vol. 11). New York: WW Norton & Company.
8. Adorno, T. W., & Horkheimer, M. (1997). *Dialectic of enlightenment* (Vol. 15). London: Verso.

9. Lacan, J. (1977). Direction and power of treatment. In *Écrits: A selection* (pp. 250–310).

10. Lacan, *The four fundamental*, p. 276.

11. Klein, N. (2015). *This changes everything: Capitalism vs. the climate*. New York: Simon and Schuster, p. 23.

12. Anderson, B. (2006). *Imagined communities: Reflections on the origin and spread of nationalism*. London: Verso Books.

13. Lacan, J. (1977). The mirror stage as formative of the function of the I as revealed in psychoanalytic experience. In *Ecrits*.

14. Žižek, S. (1992). *Looking awry: An introduction to Jacques Lacan through popular culture*. Cambridge: MIT press, p. 162.

15. Ibid.

16. Ibid., p. 165.

17. Ibid.

18. Ibid.

19. Lacan, *The four fundamental*, p. 46.

20. For an extended critique of Zizek's politics, see my Samuels, R. (2010). *New media, cultural studies, and critical theory after postmodernism: Automodernity from Zizek to Laclau*. New York: Palgrave, pp. 187–199.

21. Žižek, S. (2009). *The parallax view*. Cambdridge: MIT press, pp. 29–30.

22. Klein, *This changes*, p. 25.

23. Horkheimer, *Dialectic of enlightenment*.

24. Bleicher, J. (2014). *The hermeneutic imagination (RLE Social Theory): Outline of a positive critique of scientism and sociology*. New York: Routledge.

25. Pinker, S. (2003). *The blank slate: The modern denial of human nature*. New York: Penguin.

26. Lacan compares psychoanalysis to the free discovery of knowledge in opposition to academic discourse in his *The Four Fundamental Concepts*, p. 260.

27. See Samuels, R. (2014). *Between philosophy and psychoanalysis: Lacan's reconstruction of Freud*. New York: Routledge.

28. Lacan, J., & Miller, J.A. (2013). *The ethics of psychoanalysis 1959–1960: The seminar of Jacques Lacan*. New York: Routledge.

29. Klein, *This changes*, p. 39.

30. Ibid., p 40.

31. Ibid. p. 48.

32. Ibid., p. 52.

33. Bloom, P. (2014, 10 September). Against empathy. *Boston Review.*, https://bostonreview.net/forum/paul-bloom-against-empathy. Accessed April 2016.

34. Chodorow, N.J. (1989). *Feminism and psychoanalytic theory*. New Haven: Yale University Press.

35. Laclau, E. (2012). *Politics and ideology in Marxist theory*. London: Verso.

36. Klein, *This changes*, p. 61.
37. Žižek, S. (1992). *Looking awry: An introduction to Jacques Lacan through popular culture*. Cambridge: MIT press.
38. Laclau, E. (2005). *On populist reason*. London: Verso, pp. 232–239.
39. Klein, *This changes*, p. 63.
40. Ibid., 1 pp. 56–57.
41. Martin, A. *Empire files*. https://www.youtube.com/watch?v=PV_PLCC6jeI. Accessed May 2016.
42. Klein, *This changes*, p. 82.
43. Ibid., p. 95.
44. Ibid., p. 118.
45. Mark Bracher (2009) critiques this extremism and binary logic of the Left in his *Radical pedagogy: Identity, generativity, and social transformation*. (New York: Macmillan).
46. Klein, *This changes*, p. 170.
47. Freud, S. (1963). The economic problem of masochism. In *General psychology*. New York: Collier Press.
48. Freud, S. (1969). *Beyond the pleasure principle*. J. Strachey (Ed.). New York: Norton.
49. Gutiérrez, N., (ed.). (2007). *Women, ethnicity, and nationalisms in Latin America*. New York: Ashgate Publishing, Ltd.
50. Assembly, U.G. (1948). Universal declaration of human rights. *UN General Assembly*.
51. Laclau, E. (2005). *On populist reason*. New York: Verso, pp. 69–71.
52. Stiglitz, J.E. (2002). *Globalization and its discontents*. New York: Norton.

CHAPTER 6

Conclusion

Abstract Psychoanalysis offers an important way of challenging contemporary politics and offering a path toward global solidarity. I have argued that the stress on the neutrality of the analyst and the process of free association help us to think beyond the victim identification of the Right and the obsessional narcissism of the liberal Left.

Keywords Solidarity · Neutrality · Freud · Lacan · Zizek · Evolution · Biology · Cynical conformity · Ego psychology · Enjoyment · The Other

Psychoanalysis offers an important way of challenging contemporary politics and offering a path toward global solidarity. I have argued that the stress on the neutrality of the analyst and the process of free association help us to think beyond the victim identification of the Right and the obsessional narcissism of the liberal Left. At a time when the new discourses of neuroscience and evolutionary psychology seek to impose a biological solution to every mental problem, the importance of psychoanalysis only increases, and yet, the practice that Freud founded is being undermined from both within and without. Not only do insurance companies steer practitioners to adopt a medical model, but psychoanalysts themselves have turned to counter-productive theories stressing biology and "normal" communication. The radical nature of psychoanalysis is therefore being lost in a

© The Author(s) 2016
R. Samuels, *Psychoanalyzing the Left and Right After Donald Trump,*
Critical Theory and Practice in Psychology and the Human Sciences,
DOI 10.1007/978-3-319-44808-4_6

discourse of cynical conformity. In this social setting, Lacan's critique of American psychoanalysis and culture is particularly relevant.

Throughout his early work, Lacan sought to distinguish American ego psychology and "the American way of life" from Freud's groundbreaking discourse. For example, in his early text "Aggressivity in Psychoanalysis," Lacan critiques contemporary society in the following way: "It is clear that the promotion of the ego today culminates, in conformity with the utilitarian conception of man that reinforces it, in an ever more advanced realization of man as individual, that is to say, in an isolation of the soul ever more akin to its original dereliction."[1] Lacan, here, clearly ties the American version of psychoanalysis, ego psychology, to the American culture of narcissistic conformity. Throughout his work, he insists that post-Freudian psychoanalysts tend to focus attention on the relation between the reality-testing ego of the analyst and the reality-testing ego of the patient, and this form of analysis posits that analysis ends when the patient identifies with the ego of the analyst.[2]

Against the discourse of conformity and individualism, Lacan's early work focused on the decentering aspects of language, sexuality, and the unconscious, and it is this emphasis on the Symbolic Other that I have tied to the possibility of global human rights beyond the pathologies of the Right and the Left. However, it is important to point out that Lacan's later work and the writings of many of his followers represent a tendency to privilege what I will call a libertarian nihilism. In seminars like *Encore*, Lacan stresses the way patients identify with their own drives and enjoyment (jouissance) and how this form of sexual pleasure represents a break with the social Other. Just as Freud turned to a biological explanation of the death drive in his later work, Lacan uses the concept of enjoyment to privilege the autoerotic over the social and the Real over the Symbolic. We can consider this emphasis on enjoyment and the lack of the Symbolic Other as feeding libertarian nihilism because, as Zizek claims, this type of enjoyment is idiotic and repetitive, and instead of the super-ego representing a call to submit to the social order of law and language, the central command is to enjoy.[3] Consumer capitalism, therefore, invites us to a form of libertarian nihilism where one is freely forced to find one's desire in meaningless enjoyment, and just as Margaret Thatcher said society does not exist, the later Lacan argues that the social Other does not exist since we are all driven by autistic, autoerotic enjoyment. From this perspective, Lacan's later work and Zizek's discourse can be read as reinforcing the status quo by moving from an emphasis on social language to drives, the Real, and individualistic enjoyment.

To save psychoanalysis from itself and promote a more just political order, concerned global citizens have to return to the neutrality of the analyst and the promotion of free association. As Lacan argued in the middle stage of his work, free association is never free since it always is determined by the structure of language and the relationship between previous memories and thoughts.[4] A parallel to this theory of free association can be found in Marx's idea that people make history, but they do not make it under the conditions of their choosing.[5] In other words, we do have the possibility to change the social world, but we can only do it if we clearly recognize the current structures and restraints. Therefore, from the position of analytic neutrality, we have to have an open public discourse concerning social and political issues, but the goal should be the formation of universal principles and rights and a government to protect them. It is also important to stress that with new media, we are seeing governments' and politicians' secret communications exposed in a form of free association. For example, WikiLeaks provides the opportunity to see what is being hidden from the public, and this may force political officials to be more forthcoming in the future.

What we can take away from Lacan's later work is the notion that the Other, as the larger Symbolic order, does not exist in the sense that there is no predetermined moral order or divine order or even natural order. Humans make their own order, and thus, humans can change that order, but what we need to do in order to complete the project of the Enlightenment is to establish secular humanism as the counter discourse to religious and political ideology. Instead of relying on some idealized and fantasied Other to save us, we need to remember how people working together have transformed the social world.

In terms of contemporary global social justice movements, one possibility for empowerment is for people to realize that they have been transformed from citizens into consumers. By understanding this shift, consumers from all over the world can work together online and claim their new power by participating in mass, global boycotts of particular products and companies. In a new mode of the master-slave dialectic, large multinational corporations are reliant on consumers to buy their products and to promote their brands, and if people rebel against these companies, consumers can hold them hostage to particular demands. Since these corporations have gone global, we must also create a global form of citizen power to force these companies to accept a new world order.

Of course, the most likely scenario for change will occur after a global financial or environmental crisis, but it may be too late then to save our world. What we saw after the financial crisis of 2008 was the ability of the global financial class to save themselves as they watched millions of people slip into poverty. It appears that very little has been learned from this crisis, and yet, we are also seeing the push for a real Left alternative, but as I have stressed, this alternative is limited by sticking to the nation-state and not seeing the need for a global solution. One result of failing to call for a global system of government is that every economic crisis is blamed on immigrants since they are seen as disruptive outsiders; however, if we are able to form a global sense of solidarity, we can reduce this Right-wing attraction to scapegoating the other.

Ultimately, it is wrong for me to propose a specific path toward our future global government because I have argued that psychoanalysis teaches us to move beyond the need for the idealized person who knows the truth. Furthermore, post-Marxist theorists have stressed that there is not an inevitable path of history, and as Zizek has argued, contingent decisions only become necessary after the fact: in other words, we only know the path of history after it has been accomplished, and from this retrospective position, everything seems necessary, but in reality, there are always choices to be made and the future is undefined and open. Since people make history, but they do not make it under conditions of their choosing, we have to understand how our political and economic systems function as we refuse to believe in a savior who has all of the answers. Only organized collective action will make sure that the new global order is democratic and just.

NOTES

1. Lacan, J. (1977). *Ecrits* (trans: Sheridan, A.). New York: Norton, p. 27.
2. Lacan, J. (1981). *The four fundamental concepts of psychoanalysis.* (trans: Sheridan, A.), Miller, J. A. (Ed.). New York: Norton, p. 145.
3. Žižek, S. (1992). *Looking awry: An introduction to Jacques Lacan through popular culture.* Cambridge: MIT press, p. 128.
4. Lacan, J. *The four fundamental* concepts, p. 54.
5. Marx, K., & Norman Bethune Institute. (1977). *The eighteenth brumaire of Louis Bonaparte.* Moscow: Progress Publishers.

INDEX

© The Author(s) 2016
R. Samuels, *Psychoanalyzing the Left and Right After Donald Trump*,
Critical Theory and Practice in Psychology and the Human Sciences,
DOI 10.1007/978-3-319-44808-4

CPSIA information can be obtained
at www.ICGtesting.com
Printed in the USA
BVHW04*0220190318
510948BV00008B/38/P

9 783319 448077